QUANTITATIVE METHODS

AN APPROACH TO
SOCIO-ECONOMIC GEOGRAPHY

W. V. TIDSWELL, M.A.

PRINCIPAL LECTURER AND HEAD OF THE GEOGRAPHY DEPARTMENT, HEREFORD COLLEGE OF EDUCATION

AND

S. M. BARKER, M.A.

UNIVERSITY TUTORIAL PRESS LTD

9-10 GREAT SUTTON STREET, LONDON, E.C.1

Published 1971

ISBN: 0 7231 0518 9

PRINTED IN GREAT BRITAIN BY UNIVERSITY TUTORIAL PRESS LTD, FOXTON, NEAR CAMBRIDGE

PREFACE

Geographers have always lived in a world of change and the past decade has witnessed one of the more significant up-surges both in fundamental thinking and in methods of approach. It is our aim in this book to explore the new opportunities presented by current trends and equally to assess their limitations.

Professor Haggett suggests that the historian may look back upon the 1960's as a decade of mathematical extravaganza, and for many of us this has proved an alarming experience. It is hoped this book will bring techniques, which may be relevantly applied at sixth form and college levels, within the comprehension of the non-mathematician. Despite weaknesses, such techniques provide both an intellectually more rigorous approach to the immense and complex problems of modern society, within which geography seeks to find a pattern and order, and more interesting ways of learning.

Quantitative techniques enable a more accurate description and penetrating analysis of the landscape to be accomplished, especially in the more nondescript regions which have hitherto defied interpretation. Traditional elements, materials, and data are used in new ways. Model theory presents a structured framework within which problems may be isolated and investigated in a scientific way. Hypotheses may be formulated and tested, rather than facts amassed, and this approach is extended into ideas for fieldwork.

For each topic current theories are examined, an illustrated example given, and practical exercises set. Full instructions are given for difficult or less familiar work, but simpler methods are not so elaborated. Although compartmentalised, the divisions are purely expedient and the evident relationship between chapters is that of locational description and analysis. An appendix of mathematical formulae is included, together with an extract of random numbers. Sources of published data readily available to geographers may be found in Appendix I, which has been kindly compiled by Alan Hammersley of S. Katharine's College, Liverpool.

Gratitude is owed to many who have contributed to the writing of this book. The springboard of many ideas was the stimulating series of courses directed by Professor Peter Haggett and Richard Chorley at Madingley Hall, Cambridge. Students have worked patiently and helped modify numerous exercises. Readers in university, college, and school have generously given their time to make helpful improvements, and in particular I wish to thank Michael Chisholm, University of Bristol; Kevin Hickman, Hereford College of Education; Michael Carr, Homerton College, Cambridge; and David Money of Bedford School. To my co-author, Sheila Barker, I am grateful, not only for her written contribution on agriculture, but for her stringent, constructive criticism of my own work in its formative stages.

I am indebted to the Director General of the Ordnance Survey and the Controller of H.M. Stationery Office for permission to reproduce the maps of Hereford and Taunton areas, to Messrs Bartholomew & Son for the map of the Lincoln area, and to Miss Alice Coleman for the Land Utilisation Map. My thanks are also due to those writers and publishers who have kindly given me permission to use or adapt diagrams from their publications, diagrams that are individually acknowledged in the text.

Little is ever achieved without the loyal support of one's own family. The generosity of my wife, Patricia, who has read the manuscripts at various stages to ensure clarity of explanation and arithmetical accuracy, in addition to coping with the common round of domestic life, has been boundless. To her I am especially grateful.

Hereford. 1970   VINCENT TIDSWELL.

CONTENTS

QUANTITATIVE METHODS

AN APPROACH TO SOCIO-ECONOMIC GEOGRAPHY

CHAPTER 1

INTRODUCTION TO MODELS AND QUANTITATIVE TECHNIQUES

The Scientific Method of Enquiry. Models. Quantitative Techniques.

Geography is concerned with the search for order in the complex and ever-changing patterns in space and to offer some rational explanation of them. Such patterns are complex not only because of the diversity of landscape in both environmental and human terms but also because of the time through which it is evolving. In the past we have been too concerned with regional differentiation or the uniqueness of regions—the so-called **idiographic** studies—and too concerned with seeking causes within the physical environment. That such an approach is inadequate in the analysis of the contemporary scene is highlighted in extracts from the writings of C. A. Fisher and A. Cairncross as quoted in Chisholm: *Geography and Economics:* "Of course the assessment of the part played by the factors of the physical environment is supremely important, alike as a practical and philosophical problem, but a balanced answer will never be obtained until we are willing to give appropriate weight in our considerations to all relevant factors. Either we must stop pretending to be causal geographers or else we must honestly seek the right causes". (C. A. Fisher.)

"Suppose, for example, that we ask why some industry—say shipbuilding—has become localised on the Clyde. We really have two questions to answer, not one. First, why the Clyde rather than some other place—the Thames or the Severn? Second, why shipbuilding rather than some other industry—steel or textiles? We have to show, not only that there is a pull on shipbuilding to the Clyde, but that the pull is *relatively* greater than the pull on other industries." (A. Cairncross.)

How far we have fallen short, not only of finding answers to such imponderable questions posed by these writers, but also of structuring an adequate method of investigation is clear from the report of the Sixth Form and University Standing Committee of the Geographical Association published in *Geography*, Vol. 53, Part 1, January, 1968. To try to "seek the right causes" in a sophisticated society it is necessary to move beyond the earth sciences, for so long the basic platform of school geography, towards the social sciences and to the consciousness of a man-man relationship rather than a man-land one. This inevitably involves geographers in the scientific method of enquiry of which model building and the use of quantitative techniques are an intrinsic part and from which may emerge the so called **nomothetic** studies, *i.e.* where patterns repeat themselves thus enabling the deduction of principles to be made.

The Scientific Method of Enquiry

From the time of the earliest field-workers, *e.g.* the Forsters in the eighteenth century, in attempting an analysis of landscape, geographers have followed a logical sequence of events: they have made observations, recorded them, analysed results, and deduced some conclusions from the original observations. To this extent our methods of investigation have always been scientific. Why then do we need to improve our basic techniques? The scale of reality prevents observation of total phenomena, thus the accuracy of observation will depend both upon the keenness of our perceptive powers and upon what phenomena we are looking for according to some pre-conceived idea, albeit a subconscious one.

Problems associated with observation are apparent in urban fieldwork: do we map land use on the ground floor only or on all floors? Do we regard all shops as being equal in size or do we measure frontages and apportion a scale to them? Do we merely have a classification of five basic categories or a complex one as in the Census of Distribution? Clearly it is necessary to define the limits of any enquiry and these will condition the phenomena we observe and the methods used to record them. This theme is augmented and applied in Chapter 6.

If we aim at more than mere description then the course of our research leading to the discovery of relationships must be guided by a hypothesis, *e.g.* the volume of traffic on a road joining two towns will have a strong relationship to the population of these towns and the distance separating them (see Chap. 7). What are the bases of hypotheses which may be so used? Hypotheses may be derived in three ways. The first source is the existing body of data and established relationships within our own discipline, *e.g.* heathland in Britain is confined to areas over 1,000 ft. A second way is to apply in a logical way the established principles of another discipline to our distinctive geographical data: *e.g.* economic rent and its effect upon urban land use, viz. land use is more intense in the centre of cities than on the periphery (see Chap. 7). A third source may be mere intuition or hunch arising from past experience in handling data, *e.g.* the distribution of urban renewal is a random one related to the wishes of individual speculators.

The final stage of the scientific method of enquiry is the rigorous testing of stated hypotheses against the real world and in order to carry this out it is necessary to employ quantitative data and mathematical methods to determine degrees of correlation and deviation. For example, in the first hypothesis cited above it is reasonable to suppose there would be a strong correlation between heathland and land over 1,000 ft, but a deviation would be provided by the Brecklands of East Anglia. One could then refine the hypothesis into the statement "Heathland in *Highland* Britain is confined to areas over 1,000 ft" and test again. When a hypothesis has been established by empirical evidence it then becomes one of the principles of our discipline and may be applied in a general context.

The methods as outlined here have been greatly simplified and in reality one would need to postulate and test many hypotheses to solve a single problem. In the literature this process is called factor analysis or sometimes multi-variate analysis because of the many variables which are related to each other. These relationships are often expressed mathematically in correlation matrices, an example of which is cited in Chapter 4. A great aid to interpreting the complexities of the real world is the use of mathematical models as explained below.

The three stages of the scientific method of enquiry may be summarised then as:

(1) Defining the limits and aims of the enquiry.

(2) Stating a definite hypothesis to guide our mode of approach.

(3) Rigorous testing of the hypothesis against reality and which if proven leads to the emergence of principles of the discipline.

This method of enquiry permeating the whole of our approach to fieldwork and investigation of geographical problems can be very rewarding not only in terms of results but in stimulating new attitudes in students as subsequent chapters help reveal.

Models

No fully comprehensive discussion of models can be attempted in a short space, but it is hoped to provide some adequate ideas about their properties and uses and to indicate how they are used in later chapters. Every type of model so far conceived is treated fully in *Models in Geography*, edited by Chorley and Haggett.

The more one seeks a working definition of a model, the more elusive it becomes. The word "model" as used in everyday life implies a degree of perfection and often a change in scale. In the geographical context it is suggested that the term model be regarded in three ways:

(1) As a general statement which clearly describes and attempts to explain the inter-relationships between a number of variable elements, *e.g.* Von Thunen originally used one variable element, that of distance, but all his other elements such as type of terrain remained constant (see Chap. 2).

(2) As the mathematical statement of a hypothesis in which relative values are given to each of the component elements, *e.g.* Reilly's Law of Retail Gravitation (Chap. 5).

(3) As a structured idea such as the models of urban growth discussed in Chapter 6.

Any classification of models is rendered difficult by their recent proliferation but normally three main categories are recognised:

(1) The **iconic** model represents the properties of the real world and involves only a change of scale, spatial relationships remaining the same. Into this group come the hardware models (Chap. 7) together with wave tank experiments and glacier movement models in geomorphology.

(2) In the **analogue** model one property is represented by another, *e.g.* contours replace the third dimension on the topographical map. Such maps

are the basis of school geography and of the work discussed in later chapters.

(3) The third category of models are called **symbolic** models in which properties are represented by symbols, usually measured and expressed in mathematical terms, *e.g.* the simple gravity model applied in Chapter 7. It will have been noted that the degree of abstraction has increased in moving through these categories. Haggett sums up the relationship between types of models admirably in *Locational Analysis in Human Geography:* "A very simple analogy is with the road system of a region where air photographs might represent the first stage of abstraction (iconic); maps, with roads on the ground represented by lines of different width and colour on the map, represent the second stage of abstraction (analogue); a mathematical expression, road density, represents the third stage of abstraction (symbolic)".

It is also usual to distinguish between **static** models, *i.e.* those concerned with one period of time as in the Chrystaller settlement model explained in Chapter 5 and **dynamic** models which predict future patterns, *e.g.* the gravity model referred to above and simulation models containing a strong chance (stochastic) element as illustrated in a simple way in Chapter 4.

Whatever definition or classification we adopt, models have certain characteristics which it is helpful to identify. In order to build a model one abstracts from reality those features which are of particular interest to the specific problem, and thus models are selective and at best can provide a partial view of reality. The model neglects certain elements so that it may concentrate on others, hence the need for the builder to have skill in constructing his model—skills founded upon a sound basis of existing geographical knowledge. The more complicated models are closer to reality and one may compare the values of those of Reilly and Huff as contained in Chapter 5.

A second characteristic is their structured nature in which relationships are clearly stated. This structure, however, is dynamic in that it can be readily modified as a result of testing against reality, *e.g.* in the early literature the simple gravity model (Chap. 7) merely employs the distance between two towns, later editions employ the square of the distance whilst more sophisticated versions add an exponent to reflect not merely physical distance but the time taken to traverse it. A final feature is their predictive nature as indicated in the unsophisticated example of a simulation model contained in Chapter 3.

It is our concern as geographers to seek an order in the spatial patterns of the real, complex environment. Yet it has already been acknowledged that the scale of reality is too great to handle and its complexity too diverse to comprehend. In what ways then do models help our task? The model through its selectivity, enables us to isolate the problem and its component factors—irrelevancy or "noise" as it is now called is eliminated. The scale and complexity of reality are thus reduced and our understanding of it helped. Their structured nature provides a theoretical framework within which hypotheses may be formulated and tested as part of a sound scientific enquiry, *e.g.* Chrystaller's Settlement Model. Deviation from the expected may be noted and investigated, so the direction of further enquiry is indicated by the model, saving valuable time. The model may reveal an order in the pattern enabling us to generalise and eventually predict patterns. This prediction of future distributions is very much the concern of the geographer in the functional society of to-day. Perhaps their greatest value is that so succinctly stated by Haggett: "Models are made necessary by the complexity of reality. They are a conceptual prop to our understanding and as such provide for the teacher a simplified and apparently rational picture for the classroom, and for the researcher a source of working hypotheses to test against reality. They convey not the whole truth but a useful and apparently comprehensible part of it."

Quantitative Techniques

Quantitative and qualitative are terms much in fashion but they remain ugly adjectives. Unless we are on our guard they may become the elder sisters of Cinderella whom we may use to symbolise Geography. To keep our perspective is all important and we are reminded of this in *Geography's Balance Sheet* by Henderson.

A *qualitative* statement is one in which no scale of values is given to its parts, *e.g.* a high-class residential district is one in which there are detached and semi-detached houses. A *quantitative* statement would attach a measured value to the two components, *e.g.* a high-class residential district is one in which 80 per cent. of the houses are detached and 20 per cent. semi-detached (Chap. 6). The mathematical nature of models requires more precisely measured data than has been hitherto employed and hence the current emphasis upon quantitative techniques to fulfil this need.

Statistical methods have been the concern of geographers for many years and simple examples include: frequency diagrams, graphs, and flow line maps. To use the sources of data as outlined in

Appendix 1 to fullest advantage, it is necessary to extend the use of such methods which result in both more accurate description and penetrating analysis. Perhaps their greatest value is the revealing of relationships between phenomena which may have been suspected, but certainly not proved or evaluated. Another important application is that authentic sampling techniques reduce the scale of problems yet enable valid generalisations to be made. None of the techniques included here is difficult to manipulate, yet the user will be able to: (1) appreciate the value of sampling and apply the methods to his own problem (Chaps. 2 and 6); (2) establish intensity of farming (Chap. 2) and concentration of industry (Chap. 4) within a region; (3) calculate simple correlations to establish the strength of a relationship between two phenomena (Chap. 6); (4) analyse settlement patterns and suggest urban spheres of influence (Chap. 5).

No attempt has been made to include multivariate analysis or matrix algebra which are quite beyond the scope of school geography. The computer's contribution in geography is fully stated in *The Computer and Geography* by Hagerstrand.

There is no dichotomy between the so-called qualitative and quantitative geography—the one is an extension of the other. Statistics have been described as a powerful aid to judgement and the techniques they employ are not an end in themselves; they only become relevant when applied to problems. For this reason the analysis of real situations has been deliberately selected as the theme for this text. Galbraith's warning quoted by Rutherford has been heeded: "The proper approach for the researcher is to say, 'Here is an important problem. Which tools can be used most effectively and appropriately in solving it?' Instead, many of our research people have been saying, 'Here is a prestigious tool. Where can I find a problem or some data on which to use it?'."

Wrigley reinforces this when he writes, "Perhaps the most sensible attitude now as at other times to adopt towards the question of method in Geography is to be eclectic—to use whichever method of analysis, Blachian or systematic, landscape or Loschian, appears to offer the best hope of dealing with the problem in hand."

SUGGESTIONS FOR FURTHER READING

1. Chorley and Haggett, Ed. *Frontiers in Geographical Teaching*. Methuen, London, 1965. Especially Chapters 1 and 6.

2. Rutherford, Logan, and Missen. *New Viewpoints in Economic Geography*. Harrap, Sydney, 1966. Chapter 1.

3. Yeates. *An Introduction to Quantitative Analysis in Economic Geography*. McGraw Hill, New York, 1968. Chapters 1 and 2.

4. Chorley and Haggett, Ed. *Models in Geography*. Methuen, London, 1967. Chapters 1 and 14.

5. Chisholm. *Geography and Economics*. Bell, London, 1966. Chapter 1.

6. McCarty and Lindberg. *Preface to Economic Geography*. Prentice Hall, New Jersey, 1966. Chapters 3 and 4.

7. "Report of the Sixth Form and University Standing Committee of the Geographical Association." *Geography*, Vol. 53, Part I, 1968.

8. Gregory. *Statistical Methods and the Geographer*, Longmans, London, 1963.

9. Siegel. *Non-Parametric Statistics*. McGraw Hill, Tokyo, 1956.

10. Henderson. "Geography's Balance Sheet." *Transactions of I.B.G.*, No. 45, September, 1968, pp. 1-9.

11. Hagerstrand. "The Computer and the Geographer." *Transactions of I.B.G.*, No. 42, December, 1967, pp. 1-19.

12. Ambrose. *Analytical Human Geography*. Longmans, London, 1969. Chapters 1 and 2.

13. Cooke and Johnson. *Trends in Geography*. Pergamon, London, 1969. Chapters 1 and 8.

14. Walford. *Games in Geography*. Longmans, London, 1969. Chapters 1 and 2.

CHAPTER 2

AGRICULTURE

Land use maps: general comment. The von Thünen model. Economic rent. Modifications of von Thünen. Suggested exercises: testing von Thünen; use of set theory; point sampling; line sampling; distance index. Techniques in farm studies. Game theoretical models.

As a result of the essentially extensive character of agricultural activities throughout the inhabited world, agriculture in a wide variety of forms appears to dominate the pattern of land use. The range and complexity of the crop and livestock combinations, and the economic systems under which they operate makes the search for a rational understanding of the principles determining agricultural land use one which has occupied the attention of economists since von Thünen, and the ideal theory capable of universal application is still lacking.

Fundamental to this search for rational patterns in agriculture is the existence of precise and accurate data, and this is provided either in the form of agricultural statistics on a parish or county level, or in the Land Utilisation maps available in Britain on several scales. An extract from the second Land Use Survey at scale of 1 : 25,000 is included in this book as it is probably the most useful and easily available of the land use sheets for work in schools. Its merits lie in the very precise information with regard to individual fields and crops over a small area, but it does not include farm boundaries, and so no indication of the size of farms and their internal organisation is given. The first edition at a scale of 1 : 63,360, while far more generalised, has advantages in the search for overall patterns at a regional level, where the existence of several towns and variety of physical features may show adjustment of crop combinations with both distance and physical change. Finally, the ten miles to one inch land use map at a national level is highly generalised and shows the much broader patterns primarily governed by the major climatic and relief divisions of the country.

British agriculture never shows regions of true monoculture—the nearest approach is in locally permanent crops such as hops—and the intricacy of crop combinations in land use maps is great; thus in the search for order geography has long dealt with the simple relationships of physical feature and agricultural land use in the interpretation of these maps. Such a relationship is readily recognised in regions of physical extremity—areas of contrasting geology, or in places showing abrupt breaks of slope, but on the vast majority of land use maps only a bewildering complexity of land use is visible defeating any attempt to find such simple relationships—a patchwork which seems without system. The extract covering the Hartlepools area has therefore been deliberately chosen from such a region where no marked physical feature can be seen to dominate the area and so afford an easy explanation of the land use, and where distributions appear to be quite random. Increasing use is now made in agricultural geography of models in the analysis of patterns, and the ways in which some of these can give direction to the study of a land use map on this scale will be elucidated in this chapter.

The von Thünen Model

In the attempt to find some principle behind the patterns of land use, reference must inevitably be made to the agricultural location theories of von Thünen, an early pioneer in the field of agricultural economics—who aimed to discover and examine the laws governing the pattern of land use. Within his time—the early nineteenth century—and experience —as a farmer near Rostock—he did recognise some pattern of land use around cities which depended on the competition between various types of agriculture for a certain area of land in relation to its distance from the city market. For clarity von Thünen made a series of assumptions which are seldom found in reality, namely an isolated state where trade was unimportant; where soil was of equal fertility; where there was a single centrally placed city and a single form of transport. Farmers were held to react uniformly and flexibly, to these conditions in deciding how to use their land. As a method of analysis the concept is still useful today, and has never been replaced by a more adequate theory of agricultural location, although the basic concept has been refined and put into the complex context of twentieth century agriculture.

Economic Rent

Von Thünen considered the controlling factor determining the use of the land to be economic rent, and in turn the primary factor determining economic rent to be transport costs. These costs in the early nineteenth century were simple—it was dominantly a horse and cart era for the transport of agricultural goods—and so the cost of movement of such goods was proportional to distance from the city market. As a result economic rent had a spatial distribution.

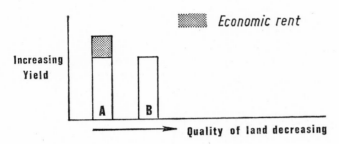

FIG. 2.1. (a)   Economic rent.

This idea is shown graphically in Fig. 2.1 (a). It must be noted that economic rent differs from the idea of rent for a house or flat; it is the surplus of production possible from using a piece of land in a certain way in comparison with using it in another way. Fig. 2.1 (b) shows the next stage of the decreasing economic rent for land at a distance from

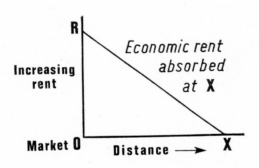

FIG. 2.1 (b).   Relation of economic rent and distance from market.

the market O. The land nearest the market commands the highest economic rent if transport costs determine the economic rent. The line R X is sometimes called the R slope, and one can easily see that the angle of this slope can vary greatly. Its steepness is governed by two main factors. First, the ease with which the total production can be transported. A bulky crop would have considerable

advantages close to the market, and so have a high economic rent, but this advantage would rapidly diminish at a distance as the cost of transport increased. Other crops with less bulk would have less obvious advantage near the market and less obvious disadvantage at a distance. Secondly, perishable goods need to be close to the central

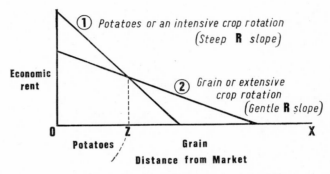

FIG. 2.1 (c).   Economic rent and distance from market: two competing land uses.

market. This was more significant in the time of von Thünen than it is to-day with the widespread use of refrigeration, yet in the case of market garden products perishability is still important in the marketing of the product.

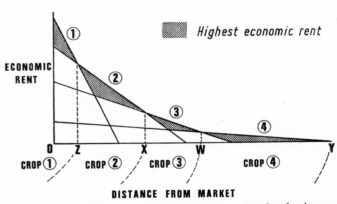

FIG. 2.1 (d).   Economic rent: numerous competing land uses.
Diagrams 2.1 (a), (b), (c), (d) based on *Rural Settlement and Land Use:* Chisholm and *A.A.G.* Vol. 57: Sinclair.

Fig. 2.1 (c) shows the next stage in the interaction of two variable R slopes with hypothetical crops 1 and 2. Again O is the market, and the line OZX shows increasing distance from the market. Here the lines of economic rent obviously cross, and from this point a perpendicular is drawn to point Z, and now the economic rent can be translated into land use. In the area near the market, *i.e.* OZ the economic rent is greater for crop 1, and the area ZX for crop 2, and so this concept of economic rent contributes to the explanation of the change in land use at point Z.

Fig. 2.1 (*d*) carries the reasoning to four crops with differing *R* slopes, and shows how a pattern of land use could develop around a market. This simple pattern of concentric circles of land use around a market was developed by von Thünen—a pattern which to some extent existed in the early nineteenth century, and which persists in some areas to-day. Chisholm in *Rural Settlement and Land Use*

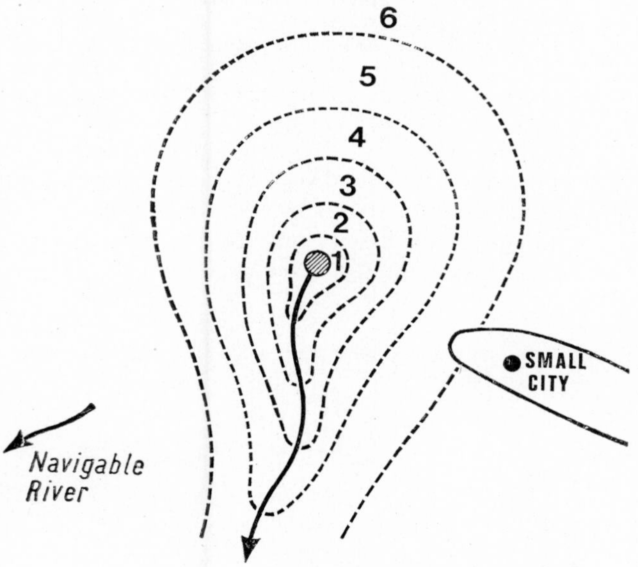

circles. Here the existence of an alternative form of transport has distorted the shape of the land use zones, because some areas equidistant from the city in mileage have differing economic rent in terms of transport costs, a factor which still operates to-day, but as a result of far more complex variables in transport media.

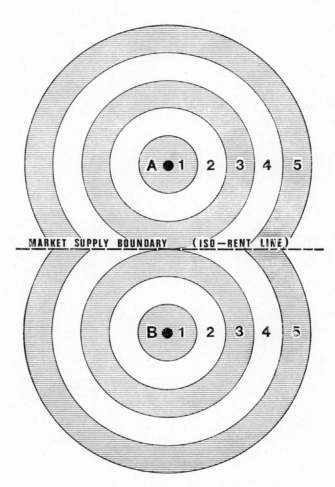

FIG. 2.2. Von Thünen. Distortion due to alternative transport and smaller city. (After Chisholm.)

Key.
1. Horticulture and dairying.
2. Sylviculture.
3. Intensive arable rotation.
4. Arable with fallow and pasture.
5. Three Field arable rotation.
6. Ranching and grazing.

FIG. 2.3 (*a*). Two markets of the same size *Source:* E S. Dunn, *Location of Agricultural Activity*, p. 60.

quotes evidence of such zoning in southern Italy, Spain, and the Punjab. Conditions have also been quoted in the 1920s in Texas, where a city market was surrounded by zones of floriculture, truck and fruit farming, dairy and poultry, grain and cotton, stock farming, and finally ranching.

This simple concentric arrangement of land use cannot appear in reality as physical features and alternative forms of transport cause complications. Von Thünen himself recognised this and produced variables in his premises—for instance, a navigable river and a neighbouring market town. The variation in the pattern thus produced is given in Fig. 2.2 in preference to the diagram of concentric

So von Thünen envisaged the development of these six zones, showing a decreasing intensity of land use with distance from the market. Horticulture and dairying due to perishability are close to the market—a commonly cited principle of modern geography. The zone of sylviculture, of course, does not exist to-day, but the location of such a zone was logical in a wood using and burning age when one considers the bulky nature of firewood and lumber. This zone is followed by the field crops with decreasing levels of intensity in production, and finally the most extensive form of land use—grazing.

Modifications of von Thünen

There are several ways in which this basic theory can be modified and developed, so giving greater links with the reality of agricultural patterns, without losing the fundamental tenets of the theory. First there is the question of multiple markets. Von Thünen envisaged only a single market where a producer could sell, but in reality there are many central markets, and production from a given area can be

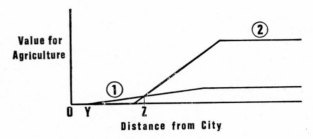

city the basic von Thünen theory may show inverse relationships in the intensity of agricultural production, which is shown diagrammatically in Figs. 2.4 (*a*) and (*b*). Von Thünen postulated a static city, where-

FIG. 2.4 (*a*). Inverse relationships around expanding urban areas.
Source: Sinclair, *A.A.A.G.*, Vol. 57, 1967, "von Thünen and Urban Sprawl".

Rings here may broaden to compensate for the loss of a supply area to **B**

FIG. 2.3 (*b*). Two unequal markets. *Source:* Dunn, p. 62.

sent to more than one of them. This is particularly important in the highly urbanised parts of the world where markets are so close together that all but the innermost zones are eliminated. Fig. 2.3 (*a*) is a highly diagrammatic representation of two market areas *A* and *B* which are sufficiently close together to displace the outer zones 4 and 5, but where forces are acting with the same strength, so maintaining the symmetrical zoning pattern. The idea is developed in Fig. 2.3 (*b*) with a dominant market *A* and a subsidiary *B*, where the supply area of *B* appears as a "wedge" disturbing the other market area. In this way the original simple patterns are destroyed, yet it does not follow that all order and system is destroyed —it has merely become more complex.

Secondly, it has been argued that around a modern

as urban growth in this century is accelerating at an unprecedented rate. In terms of value for agriculture the land closest to the city market does not have the highest value (potential sale for urban development is

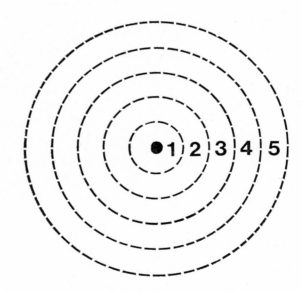

FIG. 2.4 (*b*). Zones around expanding urban areas.
Key.
1. Urban farming, 2. Vacant grazing, 3. Field crop and grazing, 4. Dairying and field crop, 5. Specialised field grain and livestock.
Source: Sinclair, *A.A.A.G.*, Vol. 57, 1967.

another question), since farmers anticipate urban growth and may not wish to invest capital, therefore the intensity of agriculture may actually increase with distance from the city. A zone of little used land has been observed quite frequently around many mid-western cities of the U.S.A.

Thirdly, it is necessary to work from the von Thünen simplification that an agricultural "ring" or zone of production is engaged in producing a single agricultural product. In reality farmers makes the recognition of zones considerably more complex as crops *A* and *B* are constant, but it does not invalidate the basic assumption that there is some order in the apparently random land use patterns. This will be illustrated in an exercise from the map extract later in the chapter.

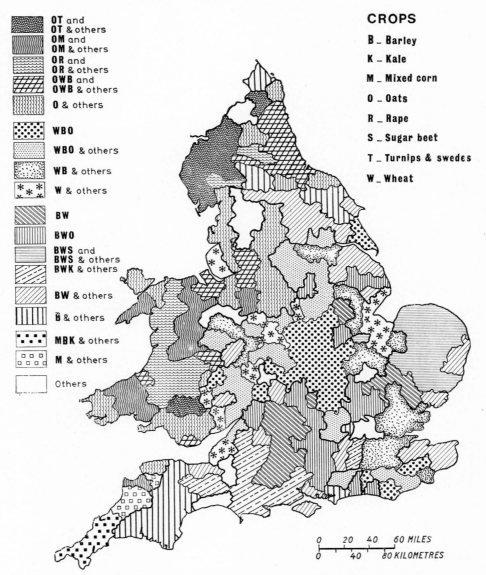

CROPS

B _ Barley

K _ Kale

M _ Mixed corn

O _ Oats

R _ Rape

S _ Sugar beet

T _ Turnips & swedes

W _ Wheat

Legend:

OT and OT & others
OM and OM & others
OR and OR & others
OWB and OWB & others
O & others

WBO
WBO & others
WB & others
W & others

BW
BWO
BWS and BWS & others
BWK & others
BW & others
B & others

MBK & others
M & others

Others

0   20   40   60 MILES
0   40   80 KILOMETRES

FIGS. 2.5 (*a*) and 2.5 (*b*). Crop combinations in England and Wales.
J. Coppock, "Crop livestock and enterprise combinations in England and Wales." *Ec. Geog.*, 1964.

operate through crop-combinations or combinations of crops and livestock. Any one zone may represent any number of products in combination, and any one crop may appear in several zones. However, at any point where a combination such as *ABC* is replaced by *ABD*, strictly a new zone is established. This

The ways in which crops are combined in British farming has recently been subjected to intense analysis by computer, and the whole country divided into regions or zones of production on this basis as shown in Figs. 2.5 (*a*) and (*b*). This data does not include grassland which is present in all combinations. Such an analysis of data on a national level is highly generalised and does not include the total range of crops actually produced, therefore on a county or parish level minor variations would undoubtedly show.   Land use maps such as the extract provide a good deal of information for the compilation of such combinations, but supplementary information would

by any map is not homogeneous, and transport costs have declined in relation to other agricultural costs, and are no longer simply proportional to distance and bulk.   There is rarely a single local market—towns are close together and expanding in a way unknown to von Thünen, and in a densely populated country such as Britain only the innermost zones are likely

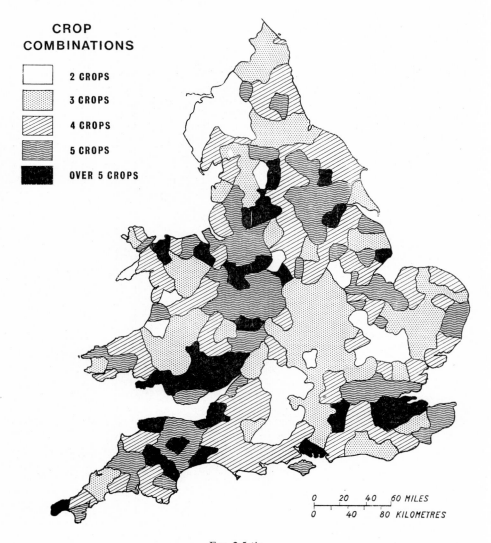

FIG. 2.5 (b).

need to be obtained from Parish Agricultural Statistics.

Von Thünen and Land Use Maps

   Before one can consider the possibility of testing the broad concept of this theory against the reality of a land use map, some comment must be made on the limitation of the work.   Obviously the area covered

to remain, as part of a macro-pattern involving the British Isles as a whole or including the continent of Europe.   Finally land use near towns is increasingly controlled by government planning.   The 1: 25,000 scale of the maps also places limitations, as insufficient area is shown on any one map to pick up variations in land use—only the juxtaposition of a whole series of sheets could show emergent patterns.

For any one land use map the initial stage in any attempt to elucidate zones is to examine the probable deviations from the model and the following com-

FIG. 2.6 (a). Sketch map of Hartlepools area.

ments apply to the extract, which is not an area of strong relief, and in terms of modern agricultural techniques can be almost regarded as homogeneous; the only steep slopes occupy a very small proportion

transport system is a dual one, but the small number of stations on the railway would render this medium of transport less important than roads. The town to some extent forms a single market as there is no significant competing centre as shown in Fig. 2.6 (a), which illustrates the spatial relationship with Middlesbrough and Newcastle conurbations. This juxtaposition of towns must have eliminated all but the inner zones, and would seem therefore to place the map within the zone of "urban and factory farming" or "horticulture and dairying". Finally, for simplicity one must assume that farmers collectively will act to maximise profits and respond in a similar way to economic stimuli. A land use map in no way purports to show yield of crops or efficiency of farming.

EXERCISE 1.   Testing von Thünen: Map 4.

On the 1 : 25,000 map the kilometre grid forms a useful basis for sampling in many ways, and is very quick and easy to use as it is already on the map. The map extract shows 54 grid squares, and it can be quickly counted that in these squares cereals are present in 54, root crops in 21, grassland in 54, field vegetables and market gardening in 46, and woodland in 19. By using a simple two choice matrix, merely presence or absence is noted of the activity. It is usual to indicate presence by 1, absence by 0. The extract is therefore revealed as an almost homogeneous area in that grassland and cereals are

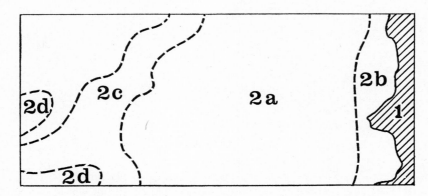

FIG. 2.6 (b).   Hartlepools extract—Sketch map (see Map 4).
Key.
1. Urban area, 2. Agricultural areas. 2(a), Core. 2(b), Core plus influence of urban.
2(c), Core plus woodland. 2(d), Core minus proportion of field crops and market
gardening.

of the area in river valleys. Apart from these slopes and the sand dunes near the coast, and the urban area itself, the land could be regarded as tillable. The

present in all squares. Field vegetables and market gardening are present in all but the western squares of the extract, while woodland is found only in the central part of the map. From this analysis of the kilometre grid a generalised sketch map could be made as in Fig. 2.6 (*b*).

A more detailed sample can then be taken across the map extract, again recording presence by 1, and absence by 0, using now the fuller criteria given in the land use key. Table 2.1 shows this more detailed breakdown and again reveals the very considerable homogeneity of the extract. Cereals are everywhere almost up to the urban boundary; roots are less widely distributed but show a similar pattern. Field vegetables with market gardening also have a

EXERCISE 2. Set theory and use.

Such variations within the agriculture of a region can be shown diagrammatically by the use of a Venn diagram, with each element in the classification regarded as a set. The model for tropical agriculture in Fig. 2.7 (*a*) is given as an example. Any one area can be "placed" within this model by the combination of its activities. A similar model could be developed using the basic divisions of the land use key as sets, and so the Venn diagram can be used as a means of expressing and elucidating the findings of the last exercise. See Fig. 2.7 (*b*). Venn diagrams are

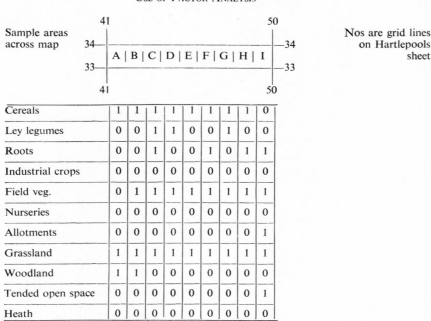

TABLE 2.1

USE OF FACTOR ANALYSIS

Sample areas across map — Nos are grid lines on Hartlepools sheet

	A	B	C	D	E	F	G	H	I
Cereals	1	1	1	1	1	1	1	1	0
Ley legumes	0	0	1	1	0	0	1	0	0
Roots	0	0	1	0	0	1	0	1	1
Industrial crops	0	0	0	0	0	0	0	0	0
Field veg.	0	1	1	1	1	1	1	1	1
Nurseries	0	0	0	0	0	0	0	0	0
Allotments	0	0	0	0	0	0	0	0	1
Grassland	1	1	1	1	1	1	1	1	1
Woodland	1	1	0	0	0	0	0	0	0
Tended open space	0	0	0	0	0	0	0	0	1
Heath	0	0	0	0	0	0	0	0	0

Characteristics of agriculture on the urban fringe are shown in Column I.

wide distribution up to the urban fringe. It is possible to determine a region with a higher percentage of woodland in the west, and on the immediate urban fringe open land is present. The nature of agriculture on the immediate urban fringe is interesting as it can reveal the changing land values which result from urban sprawl. These exercises are not devised to support the von Thünen ideas of zoning. Their purpose is merely to test something of the wider aspects of these theories against the reality of the geographical data readily available in schools. Within this framework other ideas of distance and correlation may emerge.

a very useful way of separating out hidden or "scrambled" information, and illustrating the relationships which exist between groups of objects. A series of these diagrams across a county or region can bring out small but significant changes in land use.

EXERCISE 3. Point sampling.

This technique is very fully explained in *Statistical Methods and the Geographer* by S. Gregory (Longmans).

This is a very useful technique to estimate quickly the proportions of various types of land use on any map from the sample of a series of points. Any number of points may be taken, but thirty is considered to be a minimum. If 100 points are sampled a percentage is readily available. This sample must be random, therefore random number tables must be used in conjunction with a six-figure grid reference. (See extract of random numbers on p. 79 and the instructions for their use on p. 78.)

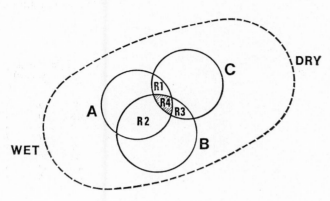

Fig. 2.7 (a). Set theory.

Key. A=Subsistence agriculture, B=Commercial cultivation, C=Herding.

Note. R1, R2, R3 are simple intersections. R4 is the intersection of 3 types.

Source: Chorley and Haggett, *Socio-economic Models in Geography,* p. 434.

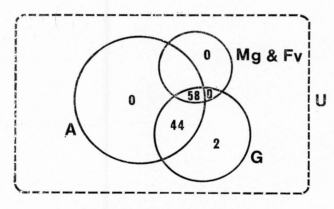

Fig. 2.7 (b). Set theory and land use.

Key. U = Universal set, A = Arable, Mg and Fv = Market gardening and Field vegetables, G = Grassland.

Note: The example uses 104 squares on the Hartlepools Sheet. The numbers represent the number of squares where the combinations occur.

Method. (1) From a table of random numbers take a six-figure reference. For example, in the following extract the first six-figure references would be 201742, 744904.

```
20 17    42 28    23 17
74 49    04 49    03 04
```

Many of these numbers will not appear on the grid actually being used—the relevant ones occur fairly infrequently.

(2) Record the land use at each of these sample points, and convert to a percentage.

(3) Determine the Standard Error for Point Sampling by applying the formula

$$\text{S.E.} = \sqrt{\frac{p \times q}{n}}$$

where p = percentage of land in a certain land use; q = percentage of land not in this land use; and n = the number of points in the sample. This error determines the reliability of the estimate afforded by the sample.

WORKED EXAMPLE USING A HUNDRED-POINT SAMPLE

Arable	Grassland	Market Gardening	Woodland	Urban
30	40	10	10	10

The percentage of arable land in the sample is 30%.

By the application of the formula for Standard Error: $\sqrt{\dfrac{30 \times 70}{100}} = \sqrt{\dfrac{2100}{100}} = \sqrt{21} = 4\cdot5$ approx.

(4) It could be stated that the percentage of arable land would be between 25·5% and 34·5% at a 68% probability level, *i.e.* one has a 68% chance of being correct. If the standard error is doubled, *i.e.* to 9 the chance of being correct is now 95%.

EXERCISE 4. Line sampling

The aim of this technique is to estimate the percentage of categories of land use in a certain area without the tedious measuring of actual area, and this can be done along each east-west grid line and each north-south grid line for a full sample. However the sample may consist of fewer lines, provided they are taken at regular intervals across the map. In this instance, using the Hartlepools map extract the east-west lines have been used as the technique may bring out some changes in land use with distance from an urban centre.

Method. This technique is worked out in detail from the Hartlepools map in Table 2.2.

(1) Along a series of east-west grid lines calculate the percentage of each category of land use, namely Arable, Pasture, Market Gardening, and Field Crops, and Woodland. To do this first measure the total length of line (14 in.). Then measure the length of the line occupied by any one category of land use, and express this as a percentage of the total line.

(2) Obtain the sample mean ($\bar{x}$) for each category of land use. In the worked example this shows grassland occupying half the area.

(3) The sample mean, $\bar{x}$, is not an accurate figure. We must now calculate the Standard Error which gives us a truer estimate of the possible range of the answer.

Having obtained from the sample the appropriate question in precise and measurable terms instead of the more usual subjective statement based on measurement by eye. In this way such samples are of considerable value to the geographer.

(2) *The greater frequency of market gardening within two miles of the urban boundary.* This can be done by taking the same six sample lines for only two miles from the edge of the built-up area, calculat-

TABLE 2.2. LINE SAMPLING

Category	Measured Lengths in each category (in inches)						Lengths expressed as percentages (x values)			
	1	2	3	4			1	2	3	4
Line 1	$5\frac{1}{2}$	6	$\frac{1}{4}$	$\frac{1}{4}$			39	43	2	2
Line 2	5	$6\frac{3}{4}$	0	$\frac{3}{4}$			36	48	0	5
Line 3	$3\frac{3}{4}$	7	$\frac{3}{4}$	$\frac{3}{4}$			23	50	5	5
Line 4	$3\frac{1}{2}$	7	1	1			25	50	7	7
Line 5	3	8	$1\frac{1}{4}$	$\frac{3}{4}$			21	57	9	5
Line 6	3	$7\frac{1}{2}$	$1\frac{1}{4}$	$\frac{1}{4}$			21	53	9	2
						Totals	165	301	32	26
					($\bar{x}$) Sample	Mean	27	50	5	4

Notes. Category   1   Arable
                      2   Grassland
                      3   Market Gardening and Field Vegetables
                      4   Woodland

Total length of line 14 in.
n is number of sample lines = 6.

In order to calculate the standard error for line sampling the following formula should be used:

$$\text{S.E.} \sqrt{\left(\Sigma x^2 - \frac{(\Sigma x)^2}{n} \right) \times \frac{1}{n} \times \frac{1}{n-1}}$$

where n = number of sample lines; x = values of a particular land use category and Σ = sum of.

Worked Example for Market Gardening and Field Vegetables

	x	x^2
Line 1	2	4
Line 2	0	0
Line 3	5	25
Line 4	7	49
Line 5	9	81
Line 6	9	81
	$\Sigma x = 32$	$\Sigma x^2 = 240$
	$(\Sigma x)^2 = 32^2$	

$$\text{S.E.} = \sqrt{\left(240 - \frac{32^2}{6} \right) \times \frac{1}{6} \times \frac{1}{5}}$$

$$= \sqrt{\frac{69}{30}}$$

$$= \sqrt{2 \cdot 3}$$

$$= 1 \cdot 5.$$

Therefore at a 68% probability level the percentage of land under market gardening and field vegetables is between 3·5 and 6·5; that is plus or minus a standard error of 1·5 from the mean of 5%.

percentages taking the map as a whole, one can then proceed to test some of the more common geographical hypotheses against this as in the following examples.

(1) *The greater frequency of market gardening along A roads.* On the extract there are 27 in. of A roads, and $4\frac{1}{2}$ in. of market gardening immediately adjacent to it which gives an approximate percentage of 17. This measurement is direct; it is not a sample, therefore no error need be calculated. The comparison of 17% with 5% (plus or minus 3 at a 95% probability level) gives an answer to this

ing the percentage in a particular land use in the same way as before, and then applying the formula for standard error. It can be calculated from the Hartlepools sheet that within two miles of the urban boundary market gardening and field crops occur with a frequency which gives a standard mean of 10% with a standard error of 4%.

EXERCISE 5.   The Distance Index

The calculation of the distance index between farm houses can be a guide to the intensity of farming in a region. It can be calculated from either a land use map or the 1:63,360 sheet together with parish agricultural statistics to cover farms not marked on the sheet. The distance index is calculated in the following way, and saves much tedious measurement on the maps of the actual distances between farms. (Source: Mather, *A.A.A.G.*, Vol. 34, 1944.)

D.I. (*i.e.* average distance from one farm to the nearest 6 farms)

$$= 1 \cdot 07 \sqrt{\frac{\text{total area involved}}{\text{total number of farms.}}}$$

e.g. Area of map 20·6 square miles. Number of farms = 4.

$$\text{D.I.} = 1 \cdot 07 \sqrt{\frac{20 \cdot 6}{4}},$$

D.I. = 1·07 × 2·27
D.I. = 2·43 miles.

intensity of the livestock rearing. The conversion table for animals into livestock units (LSU) is in Table 2.4.

This table is valuable as it gives a common unit for livestock based on the relative amount of land necessary to graze an animal. The actual amount of land needed to graze one animal varies considerably within the British Isles, from, for example, the Welsh mountains to the Cheshire plain, and so any livestock unit may need a greater or lesser amount of land. In detail there will be variations within any area as a result of differing standards of grassland management. It is difficult therefore to give a precise figure but one can consider that one livestock unit would require about 1·2 acres in good grazing country.

If, on the following hypothetical farm one wished to consider all activities in terms of their actual

TABLE 2.3

	CROPS			LIVESTOCK	
Percentage Under Tillage	Crop Combinations	Proportion Tillage Six Leading Crops		Livestock Units per 100 acres	Livestock Combinations
Farm 1. 41	W B O t p s	45 22 13 6 1		38	P S C plt.
Farm 2. 68	W S P c t o	48 30 10 7 5		20	C P plt. s

Key for crops (capitals denote importance): W/w wheat, B/b barley, O/o Oats, T/t turnips, P/p potatoes, S/s sugar beet, C/c carrots. Key for livestock: C/c cattle, P/p pigs, S/s sheep, PLT/plt poultry.

Farm Studies

Generalisations about the agriculture of a region are also derived from the micro-study of the farm as a unit, and details of individual farms are found in many regional geography textbooks. However, comparisons of farms bringing out their differing emphasis is difficult as they lack any common denominator. Modern work in the statistical comparisons of farms inputs is done by computer and quite beyond the scope of work in schools. Nevertheless, some of the principles can be applied at a simple level without the calculations becoming too tedious, and this does give a model into which farms can be placed, and from which comparisons are facilitated. The pattern in Table 2.3 is simplified from that given in *Land Use of Britain* by J. Coppock, Appendix III, and can be used for either a farm or parish.

It is important to note that livestock is treated in units and not as individual animal groups, and then given as a figure per 100 acres, which brings out the

TABLE 2.4. LIVESTOCK UNITS

Horses ..	1	Sows ..	$\frac{1}{2}$
Cows, bulls, cattle over 2 years	1	Boars..	$\frac{1}{4}$
Cattle 1-2 years	$\frac{1}{2}$	Other pigs ..	$\frac{1}{7}$
Breeding ewes	$\frac{1}{5}$	Poultry 6 months +	$\frac{1}{50}$
Rams ..	$\frac{1}{10}$	Poultry 6 months −	$\frac{1}{200}$
Other sheep ..	$\frac{1}{15}$		

acreage requirements as a common factor, the following calculations could be made.

Data		Their acreage requirements in good agricultural land would be:
Wheat	115 acres	= 115 acres
Dairy cows	80 head	80 × 1 × 1·2 = 96 ,,
Other cattle	40 ,,	40 × 0·5 × 1·2 = 24 ,,
Pigs	200 ,,	200 × 0·15 × 1·2 = 36 ,,
Sheep (ewes)	400 ,,	400 × 0·2 × 1·2 = 96 ,,

Therefore, on a basis of the percentage of total acreage requirements, wheat occupies 31% of the farm acreage, dairy cows 26%, other cattle 6·5%, pigs 10%, and sheep 26%. Therefore, given a certain number of livestock, one can calculate what proportion of the farm the livestock will need to occupy, and at least in terms of acreage it shows the emphasis in the farm activities. If one accepts the actual acreage of land in a certain use as a basis for geographical interpretation this calculation has considerable value, but to a farmer its significance is far less than the profit obtained from a particular enterprise.

It is very difficult to bring the whole field of agricultural activity to a common unit; that is to compare crops with livestock and so show the relative importance of each in a farm, parish, or region. The best method is through Table 2.5 showing man days per acre or per head of livestock per year. (A man day is the total time which would be spent by one man on any one activity in one year converted into days.)

TABLE 2.5
MAN DAYS PER ACRE OR PER HEAD

Wheat, barley, rye	..	3·5	Bare fallow	.. ..	0·5
Oats, mixed corn	..	4·5	Grass for mowing	..	2
Pulses for stock	..	4	Grass for grazing	..	0·25
Potatoes	.. ..	20	Dairy cows	.. ..	15
Sugarbeet	.. ..	17	Dairy heifers	..	9
Turnips, swedes	..	12	Beef cows	.. ..	4·5
Mangolds, fodder beet	21	Bulls	.. .. ..	7
Vegetables—brassicas	..	20	Other cattle	.. ..	3
Vegetables—pulses	..	12.5	Sows and boars	..	4
Other vegetables	..	40	Other pigs	.. ..	1·2
Hops	.. .. ..	100	Upland sheep 1 year +	0·5
Small fruit	.. ..	45	Lowland sheep 1 year +	1
Orchards with small fruit	55	Other sheep	.. ..	0·25
Other orchards..	..	25	Poultry 6 months +	..	0·3
Flowers..	.. ..	50	Poultry 6 months —	..	0·1

DATA		CONVERSION TO MAN DAYS Per acre/head			PERCENTAGE OF TOTAL
Wheat	115 acres	115 × 3·5	=	402	17%
Dairy cows	80 head	80 × 15	=	1,200	50%
Other cows	40 ,,	40 × 3	=	120	5%
Pigs	200 ,,	200 × 1·2	=	240	11%
Sheep—ewes	400 ,,	400 × 1	=	400	17%
			Total	= 2,362	

From the calculations the difficulty of determining the dominant activity on a farm can be seen. For this hypothetical data it is shown that in terms of acreage it would be classified as a predominantly grain farm, yet in terms of man days it is a dairy farm.

For the calculation of crop combination without taking into account either the livestock or the intensity of production, the calculations of J. C. Weaver are useful and simple to show changes in crop combinations. His method is based on the comparison of the actual percentage of harvested cropland in a county with the theoretical percentages. If monoculture represents 100%, then a two crop combination is 50% in each of two crops; a three crop 33·3%; and a four crop 25%, and so on. Table 2.6 is his example for a county in Iowa. (Source: J. C. Weaver, *G. Review*, **44**, 1954.)

The combination with the smallest deviation from the expected is the three-crop combination of a 309 value. In this way minor change in emphasis between neighbouring parishes and farms can be given some degree of precision. The source of data in the British Isles is the Parish Agricultural Statistics kept by the Divisional Agricultural Advisory Service.

TABLE 2.6

	1 crop	2 crops		3 crops			4 crops				5 crops				
	C	C	O	C	O	H	C	O	H	S	C	O	H	S	W
Actual percentage of cropland occupied..	54	54	24	54	24	13	54	24	13	5	54	24	13	5	2
Expected theoretical percentage	100	50	50	33⅓	33⅓	33⅓	25	25	25	25	20	20	20	20	20
Deviation from theoretical percentage ..	46	4	26	20⅔	9⅓	20⅓	29	1	12	20	34	4	7	15	18
Deviation²	2,116	16	676	427	87	413	841	1	144	400	1,156	16	49	225	323
Total	2,116	692		927			1,386				1,770				
Division by number of crops ..	2,116	346		309			347				354				

C—corn, H—hay, O—oats, S—soy beans, W—wheat.

This table can be applied to the figures given for the previous hypothetical farm, and the agricultural combinations based on man days rather than acreage requirements shown.

Game Theoretical Models

"Game theory" has developed since 1944 as an attempt to deal with the problems of optimising decisions when one has only imperfect knowledge.

The following example of Harvey (*A.A.A.G.*, **56**, 1966, p. 369) illustrates the underlying principle of game theory. Here a farmer has three possible crops, A, B, and C, which he can plant, and the income from these crops varies with only four recognised weather conditions, 1, 2, 3, and 4. The figures in the matrix represent the possible income levels he can obtain in terms of money units. This idea is fully developed in *Socio-Economic Models in Geography* (Chorley and Haggett, published Methuen, 1967), p. 448.

Broad economic principles underly agricultural geography, but it is the decision of individual farmers which determines the detail of land use in a given area. To illustrate this point, game theoretical models can be devised at varying standards of difficulty

WEATHER CONDITIONS

	1	2	3	4
Crop A	500	550	450	600
Crop B	600	700	300	600
Crop C	0	2,000	0	1,000

A West Country Farm

In this particular game it is necessary to place a class in the hypothetical situation of managing a farm in the west country for six years, and trying to maximise profits under given conditions in this period. For simplicity it is assumed that fields are of equal fertility due to the use of fertiliser, that market prices are stable, and the crop yield and therefore the profit will depend primarily on the weather during the summer of each year. On this farm the hops, blackcurrants, cider apples, and permanent pasture for hay are regarded as static, but that barley, wheat, oats, kale for cattle food, and potatoes can be grown in any quantities, in any field, although no one crop

may be repeated in the same field in any two successive years.

The profit per acre from each crop under each of the possible weather conditions can be obtained from Table 2.7. These figures are approximations only of the relative profits per acre.

The layout and acreage of the fields is as follows:

FIELD NUMBER	AREA IN ACRES	CROP
1	25	Permanent pasture
2	35	Free choice
3	30	Free choice
4	8	Blackcurrants
5	35	Free choice
6	10	Hops
7	20	Free choice
8	25	Free choice
9	10	Cider apples
10	10	Woodland
11	12	Free choice
12	15	Free choice

Procedure

(1) Choose the crops for the fields for one year and enter them on a work-sheet, following the pattern of the above table. At this stage it is not known how often or when each type of weather will occur.

(2) Shake a dice to ascertain the weather in this year.

(3) Calculate the income for each field, *e.g.* if potatoes are grown in field number 7 and the season is wet and warm, then the profit is 20 (profit per acre) × 20 (number of acres) = 400.

(4) Enter this profit against each field and add up the total profit in the year including all the "fixed" crops.

(5) Repeat for the six years in order to find the profit for the whole period.

TABLE 2.7

DICE NUMBERS

	1 Wet, warm summer	2 Dry, warm summer	3 Wet, cool summer	4 Dry, cool summer	5 Dry, cool summer, late frost May	6 Wet, warm summer, very dry harvest
Barley	9	10	7	6	6	12
Wheat	10	11	8	7	7	14
Oats	11	9	10	7	7	12
Kale	18	12	16	11	10	20
Hops	28	22	24	18	15	30
Cider apples	25	22	19	17	10	27
Blackcurrants	22	19	16	14	9	25
Permanent pasture ..	13	9	11	7	7	14
Potatoes	20	15	18	14	12	22

SUGGESTIONS FOR FURTHER READING

1. Coppock, J. T. *An Agricultural Atlas of England and Wales*, Faber, London, 1964.

2. Chorley, R. J., Haggett, P., Ed. *Socio-economic Models in Geography*, Methuen, London, 1967.

3. Chisholm, M. *Rural Settlement and Land Use*, Hutchinson, London, 1962.

4. Dunn, E.S. *The Location of Agricultural Production*, University Florida Press, Gainsville, 1954.

5. Yeates, M. *An Introduction to Quantitative Analysis in Geography*, McGraw Hill, New York, 1968.

6. Rutherford, J., Logan, M. I., Misson, G. J. *New Viewpoints in Economic Geography*, Harrap, Sydney, 1966.

7. Gregory, S. *Statistical Methods and the Geographer*, Longmans, London, 1963.

8. Hall, P., von Thünen, J. H. Ed. *Von Thünen's Isolated States* (Translation), Pergamon, Oxford, 1966.

9. Marks, R. *Simplifying Set Theory. A Programmed Text*. Bantam Pub.

10. Coppock, J. "Crop Livestock and Enterprise Combinations in England and Wales." *Economic Geography*, **40,** 1964, 65.

11. Henshall and King. "Structural Character of Peasant Agriculture in Barbados." *Economic Geography*, **42,** 1966, 74.

12. Sinclair, R. "Von Thünen and Urban Sprawl." *A.A.A.G.*, **57,** 1967, 72.

13. Weaver, J. C. "Crop Combination in the Middle West." *G. Review*, **44,** 1954, 560.

CHAPTER 3

LOCATION OF INDUSTRY

Introduction. Underlying Factors of Location and Their Importance. A Simulation Model.

Introduction

Geography is concerned with the real distribution of economic activities—with describing, analysing, and attempting to explain existing patterns at any one time. All patterns are complex but perhaps none is more puzzling to the geographer, determined to find a rational explanation, than those of industry, whether at national or local level, *e.g.* the problem posed by Cairncross about shipbuilding on the Clyde and quoted in Chapter 1, p. 1.

The reasons for such complexity are not difficult to find when it is remembered that industrial location patterns evolved throughout the centuries prior to the industrial revolution, since when growth has accelerated with every passing decade. The factors of production, in terms of raw materials and the techniques used to process these, constantly change, and each period of time leaves a residual pattern upon which are imposed later ones. This dynamism in the geographical scene is emphasised again in town growth (see Chap. 6).

The frustrations of the geographer are well summarised by the late Professor Wilfred Smith when he writes: "Distribution patterns (of industry) have been developed by trial and error, by conscious experiment and by spontaneous variation, on the part of a host of individual entrepreneurs in order to facilitate the practice of a particular economic activity". The key to the explanation of locational patterns lies not so much in the distribution of certain physical factors as in the whims and decisions, rational or emotional, of the individual. Economists in the past have assumed that such entrepreneurs would choose what is called a minimax location, *i.e.* one where costs are minimised and returns maximised, but it is now recognised that the industrialist often cannot make a decision upon this basis because of inadequate data at any one given time and the revolutionary speed at which criteria change in the present world. Many examples may be chosen from the present century to illustrate that a minimax location in 1900 is not the same as that for 1960 if only because of the advent of road transport, the electricity grid, and automation, all of which affect markets, ease of assembling raw materials, power supplies, and demand for labour.

The scale of modern industry is a further complicating factor; rarely do we find the single factory producing one product or even a group of products. Many factories form part of multiple firms with a whole range of products as in the giant chemical combines. Furthermore, the automated methods of production dictate a minimum optimum size for any given operation if scale economies are to be effective, *e.g.* a car assembly line may need to produce 60,000-100,000 cars per annum to prove competitive. This concept of the optimum size of unit is responsible for the development of subsidiary industries of which the most striking case is that of the car component firms.

The personal motives of individual industrialists, the social policies of governments, together with the inadequate and fluid costing data lead geographers away from explaining observed patterns in terms of optimum or minimax location towards a concept of satisfactory location. Could William Morris have succeeded as well in Penzance as in Cowley? Is Cowley any more or less satisfactory than Coventry? The importance of individual decisions within broad zones indicated by economic geography is the theme of this chapter in which the reader may play a positive role in the working of the simulation model.

Underlying Factors of Location and Their Importance

Although the particular site of a factory is the result of an individual decision, there are certain factors which help determine whether or not this is a satisfactory location and hence in turn the prosperity of the industry. Decisions can be disastrous, satisfactory, or very rewarding and an appreciation of some of the underlying factors provides a structure within which valid judgements may be made. The present day distribution of industry in belts or agglomerations indicates certain common factors which establish broad zones, within which an industry is most likely to succeed. Included amongst these factors are: availability of raw materials, power and labour, proximity to markets and transport. To-day two other criteria in addition to these more traditional ones are especially important: (*a*) the existing industries in the area because scale economies often dictate satellite industries and (*b*) the social policies of governments, *e.g.* incentives to move into development areas or new towns.

Raw Materials

Great emphasis has been placed in the past upon proximity to raw materials, yet Britton found in his study of the Bristol region that availability of labour and good labour relations proved to be key factors. For the pre-war factories these two factors ranked first and second in importance whilst availability of raw materials ranked sixth. For the post-war factories surveyed, availability of labour ranked first, good labour relations sixth, whilst raw materials were eleventh in order of importance. However, some account must still be taken of raw material index, *i.e.* where a heavy weight of raw materials is used in proportion to the weight of the finished product. Such industries are likely to be located near to their source of raw materials, for example, metal refining, lumbering, and sugar-beet processing. Perishable materials also attract appropriate processing industries such as the fruit and vegetable factories of East Anglia located within or adjacent to the growing areas.

Power

Power in the past has proved itself as important as the easy availability of raw materials. The changing pattern of the iron and steel industry indicates its continued importance; the Weald and Forest of Dean being premier regions when charcoal and water were sources of power, contrasting with later coalfield locations. Although the iron and steel industry in Great Britain is often quoted as the classic case of inertia it must be remembered that this force has been enhanced by the continued availability of cheap power.

To-day decentralisation of industry is helped by the mobility of electricity, especially through the high voltage national grid, whilst those ore smelting industries requiring enormous quantities of cheap power are still located in close proximity to such sources, *e.g.* H.E.P. attracts aluminium smelting whilst the processing of zinc on Severnside is favoured by the large nuclear power potential of that area. The dispersed pattern of industry in Switzerland where H.E.P. provided power in an easily transported form

contrasts with the agglomerations on the British coalfields established in the days of steam power. Whilst in the nineteenth century the effect of power was to concentrate industry into a few areas, its most significant contribution at the present time is to disperse the earlier agglomerations.

Labour

The distribution of industry in Great Britain has tended to reflect the regional skills of the population, for example, the textile industries of Yorkshire and Lancashire. It must, however, be realised that labour and plant are alternatives, and increasing automation not only decreases the number of people required but also changes the structure of employment to a bulk supply of semi-skilled machine minders and a very few really skilled people. Thus industrialists are less concerned with the number and skills of available labour than with attitudes to work and a history of good labour relations. This is again evident in Britton's study of the Bristol region. The decentralisation of the car manufacturing industry from the Midlands and the man-made fibre textile industries from Yorkshire and Lancashire indicate this growing possibility of breaking away from regions where traditional skills in these industries are to be found.

Markets

Proximity to market is yet another factor of diminishing importance except in the case of weight gaining industries such as baking and brewing. Even in these two activities the pull of the local market compared with the scale economies effected when producing for a much larger regional market is diminishing rapidly as may be deduced from the emergence of the few large multiple bakers. Equally it may be asked how many towns still retain their own local brewery? Most markets to-day are at least national in size and it is impossible to conceive the market as the fixed point of the classic economists of the past. Nevertheless, other factors being equal, it is obviously advantageous to locate so that the bulk of the market is near at hand; hence the explosive development of industry in the Midlands and south-east.

Transport

Transport is a key factor in investigating the present industrial landscape, hence an analysis of the transport network itself may well indicate areas of stagnation as well as growth points and axes (see Chap. 7). With constant improvements in both networks and means of transport, raw materials may be carried more economically for longer distances and markets become increasingly more accessible. Although freight rate structures are complex there is an overall tendency for costs per ton-mile to decrease as the distance of the haul increases, and thus together with the scale economies resulting from a larger production unit, it is often more economical to have fewer, larger factories serving larger areas, e.g. the recent mergers in the motor car and textile industries. This tendency is again emphasised at international level by current trading areas such as E.E.C. and E.F.T.A., which increase the size of potential markets.

The emergence of freight traffic on the roads during the inter-war years and its greatly expanded volume since World War II has facilitated the decentralisation of a wide variety of the so-called light industries which often occupy sites on the periphery of larger cities and are adjacent to important trunk roads. Motorways will enable the economic radius of road transport to be increased far beyond the 100 miles based upon average speeds and the controlled length of the driver's working day.

Government Policies

In sophisticated society there is often a conflict between what is socially desirable and what is economically feasible. This is wryly described by Wreford Watson as "uneconomic geography".

With the advent of nationalisation the government became one of the major employers of industrial labour in this country, yet direct intervention had begun nearly forty years ago with the Distribution of Industries Act which created special areas such as the North-east, Clydeside, and South Wales. These regions had become depressed areas largely because of their world economic situation and because of their almost complete dependence upon a single heavy industry, e.g. shipbuilding. The government attempted to attract newer light industries into these regions by offering loans to begin factories, reducing taxation and industrial rates, and by the provision of buildings and services in advance of demand. From this intervention arose the concept of the "trading estate" where all industrial services were provided on an advantageous site, e.g. the Team Valley Estate to the west of Newcastle, chosen for its proximity to the main line railway and the Great North Road.

The aim of this policy was to make the peripheral areas more attractive to the entrepreneur and so offset the locational advantages of the Midlands. This may be compared with the policy in the U.S.A.

of freight "fixing" to promote the development of the Far West, but there is one significant difference. In the U.S.A. hidden subsidies were provided to stimulate initial development whilst in Great Britain they were an attempt to try to diversify the economy in those highly specialist industrial conurbations which had grown up as a response to nineteenth-century conditions. Inertia and its consequent anachronistic pattern is perhaps the greatest impediment to development at the present time.

Government intervention operates to-day at both national and regional levels. Certain areas are designated "Development Areas" and it is interesting to note they show a marked similarity to the peripheral areas of pre-war days, and that government subsidies are being used to attract diversified industries into them. At regional level planners are concerned to relieve congestion in the conurbations, and at the same time to control the sprawl of industry into the surrounding countryside. Therefore it is common to find, as in the west Midlands, areas designated as new towns or overspill towns to form growth points, whilst others are protected as green belts.

Summary

No one factor or group of factors in isolation can offer an explanation for the present day pattern of industry; at best they provide a structured framework within which to approach the problem. The present pattern in any advanced country is inevitably complicated by the residue of a bygone decade which still exerts a continuously powerful force, that of inertia. This holds true for the communist planner in the U.S.S.R. where the urge to move industry eastwards is hampered by the existing and dominant pattern of European Russia as much as in the capitalist world. Even in a quantitative age when the industrial planner has all the advantages of the computer to help with cost benefit analyses, algorithms, and linear programmes, for finding the optimum economic answer, he may be persuaded by the government planner to re-assess the problem in human and social terms. It is suggested that decisions are usually compromise ones containing a strong chance or personal element, and it is this factor which is given prominence in the following simulation model.

A Simulation Model

No mention has been made of the conventional location theories such as those of Weber and Fetter. The reasons for this are that such theories are well described and commented upon by Alexander and in any event they can scarcely be applied in the real world. Indeed, they do much to illustrate the gulf which existed in earlier economic studies *vis à vis* geographical studies, in that few economists concerned themselves with locational patterns and few geographers with economics. Amongst the difficul-

the raw material of another. Weber, in his analysis, was concerned with the individual firm, whereas the geographer is interested in patterns of industry. Finally, the Weber model is a static model, whereas there is a continuing spatial change in supply and demand.

If it is accepted that a sound way to learn is through

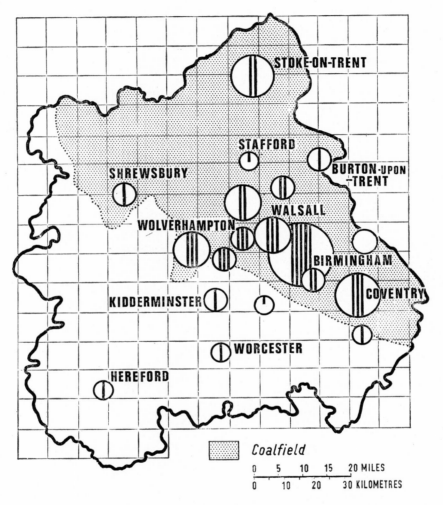

FIG. 3.1. Distribution of present-day industries. Scale of industry is indicated by size of circle and diversity by the number of bars.

ties of applying Weber's theory in the real world are: sources of raw materials and markets are regarded as fixed points not as areas, transport costs are not simply proportional to distance (freight rate structures are most complex), the framework of perfect competition is unrealistic and manufacturing is not just the processing of raw materials into finished products for the end product of one industry is frequently

experience, then, by attempting to work the simple simulation exercise which follows, the reader may well begin to appreciate the importance of (*a*) limitations of data, (*b*) how the industrialist takes a decision upon the basis of imperfect knowledge, (*c*) how the chance element may affect location decisions, and (*d*) how to predict future patterns and their likelihood of being correct.

Procedure for Working the Simulation Model

(1) *The Problem.*—Imagine that fifty new factories are to be built in the West Midlands Economic Planning Region during the next five years and you wish to predict where these factories will be built. What data would you require to make a rational assessment of this? Since you are concerned with —always the most elusive in geography—of chance or whim. This exercise is a first attempt to answer Professor Peter Hall's charge in *New Society*, that much of present school geography is folk lore and that it would be more profitable to use the computer structure afforded us by the kilometer grid to organise and record data.

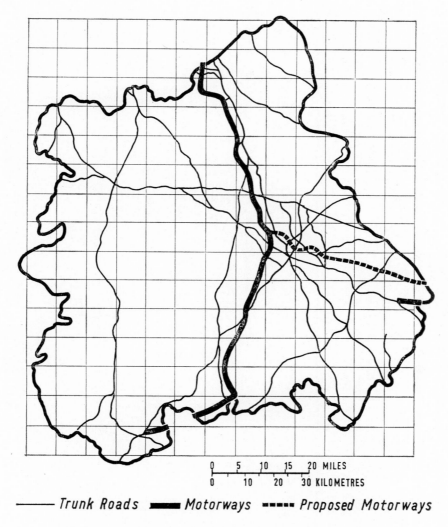

0	5	10	15	20 MILES
0	10	20	30 KILOMETRES	

———— *Trunk Roads* ■■■■ *Motorways* ▪▪▪▪▪ *Proposed Motorways*

FIG. 3.2. Major road communications in the West Midlands.

perhaps fifty industrialists of differing shrewdness and temperament, how could you ensure your prediction to be a valid one? With computer programming and sophisticated data it would be possible to predict the most likely pattern. Clearly the crude data and simple methods employed in this exercise can only illustrate the principles of decision taking upon the basis of a given body of data and the human element

(2) *The Data.*—The exercise is open-ended in that you are constantly advised to assess what you are doing as you proceed. The data provided here in map form consists of the extent of the coalfield together with the scale and range of the present industries contained within the area (Fig. 3.1), communications (Fig. 3.2), and designated areas (Fig. 3.3). All maps are covered by an identical grid. This

particular set of data has been selected as being the most significant in view of the earlier discussion of underlying principles. The distribution of the scale and range of industries indicates the ease of assembling components and semi-processed materials and the opportunity for securing the few key skilled personnel. The communications network will determine the

it. Are you satisfied with the selection of these factors as being the most important ones?

(3) *Allocation of Opportunity.*—For each grid square on the map allocate a number of points for each of these four sets of factors with the maximum for each being as follows: coalfield 2, existing industry 5, communications 8, designated areas 10. The total

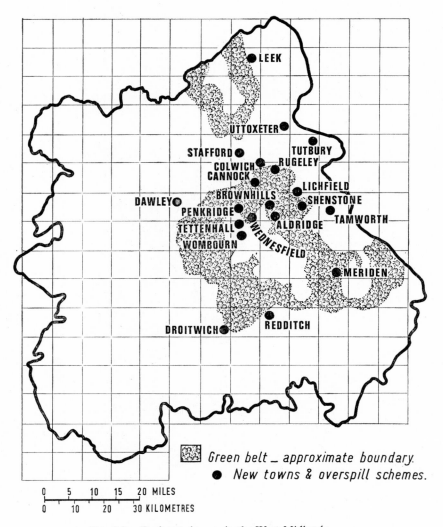

FIG. 3.3. Designated areas in the West Midlands.

ease with which raw materials may be assembled and finished products distributed. Note we are not concerned with the location of either, but with the opportunity for assembly or distribution via the transport network. Finally, a key factor will be the decision of planning authorities who at one extreme will actively encourage factory building, whilst at the other forbid

points possible for each square is thus 25. This allocation was made in the light of the earlier discussion of factors and their importance. Discuss the weighting of these factors with other members of your group and see if you agree or wish to change this, always being clear in your mind why you are altering the weighting.

For each square in turn award points for each of the four sets of factors *according to your own judgement*, placing the four sub-totals in the corner of the square as follows: minerals top left-hand corner, communications top right-hand corner, designated areas bottom left-hand corner, and present industry bottom right-hand corner. The total for the square

communications 2, present day industry 3, and coalfield 0. The total allocation is 5 out of a possible 25. Fig. 3.4 shows the points awarded to all the individual squares by one particular student.

The next step is to translate the total allocated to each square into a running total shown in Fig. 3.5.

A chance element is introduced to select locations.

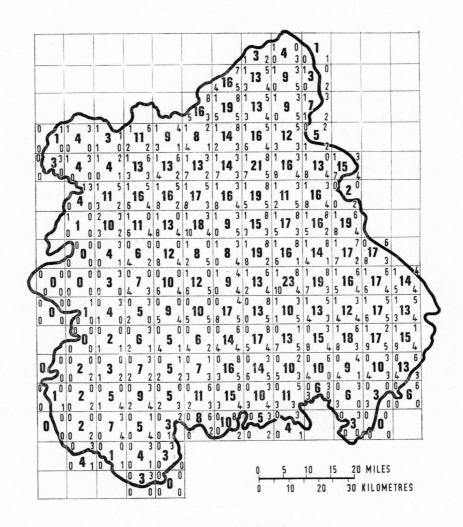

FIG. 3.4. Factor allocation.

should be placed in the middle and ringed. For example, supposing a square is located in the Green Belt, is partially served by major roads, and is located near to present-day industry of a diverse kind. Suppose too that you do not regard the presence of a coalfield as essential to modern industry. The allocation may well be: designated area 0,

Since the squares containing the greatest ranges in their running totals have the greatest chance of being selected, the weighting allocated to the various factors remains important in deciding future sites, despite the chance element. The higher the total of the square the greater the chance of its being selected.

(4) *Allocation of Factory Sites.*—Using the extract of random number on p. 79, call numbers until fifty sites for new factories have been obtained, *e.g.* if 0150 is called then the square containing 150 within its range (in this case the square numbered 150-163 on Fig. 3.5) is awarded a factory site. A pattern generated in this way by a student is shown in of other individuals in your group. If there is a marked zoning within a particular area this may well be caused by a similarity of interpretation of the broader factors as earlier discussed, operating upon the economic landscape. These factors create wide areas which may have advantages over others. Specific location sites within this favoured zone will

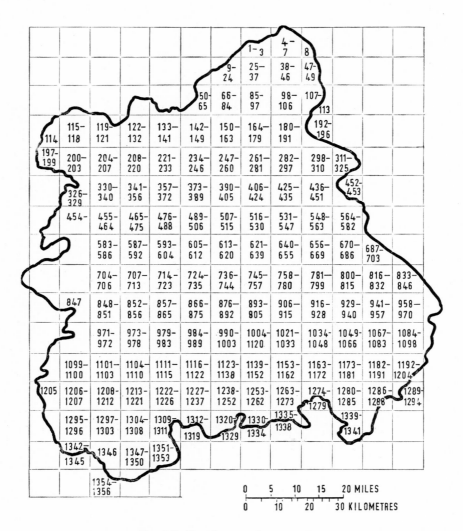

FIG. 3.5.   Random number allotment.

Fig. 3.6.   Strictly speaking, Fig. 3.4 should further be modified so that the grand total should sum to one, since probability must always sum to one (see Chap. 5, p. 47), but this step has been omitted to simplify and expedite the procedure.

(5) *Conclusion.*—Compare your results with those

depend upon the chance element—just as it does upon the particular opportunity often presented by chance to the individual entrepreneur. Once the geographer understands and appreciates this as a real and powerful influence his frustration in not finding simple answers to complex problems may be largely alleviated.

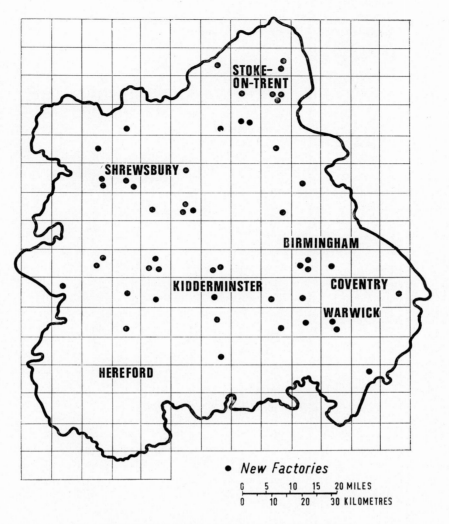

Fɪɢ. 3.6. A pattern of new industry in the West Midlands.

CHAPTER 4

PROCESSING AND PRESENTATION OF INDUSTRIAL DATA

Methods of Measuring Concentration and Specialisation; Activity Rates; Geographical Relationships.

Although the published sources of data are contained in Appendix 1, it is frequently necessary to collect and standardise original field material. A relevant questionnaire together with minimum list headings from the Standard Industrial Classification will be found at the end of this chapter.

The aims of this section are to increase accuracy of description, to enable deeper analysis, and to familiarise terms and methods employed in advanced studies of industry. It is hoped, too, that relationships may be revealed which may not be readily apparent from a visual inspection of data.

Description

The distribution of industries may be conveniently shown cartographically by circles proportionate to the number of employees, correctly located on the map. These circles may also be subdivided to indicate the proportion of workers in desired categories. Examples of such representation are found in many standard texts and the method requires no elaboration.

A growing tendency is to use a grid of squares, the size of which is dependent upon the scale of the problem and the amount of detail required in order to achieve greater accuracy. This format is also very suitable for computer programming but seems to have limited use below university graduate level at the moment. A brief explanation of the method may help reading of more advanced texts. To describe the distribution of industry in a large conurbation such as Manchester, for each grid square contained within the area calculate a location quotient by using the formula:

$$\frac{\text{Number of employees in square 1}}{\text{Total number of employees in Manchester}} \times 100$$

This would enable the detailed concentration and centres of gravity of industry in the city to be ascertained. The procedure could also be adapted to determine the degree of concentration of a particular type of industry such as jewellery in Birmingham. Although no examples are included here because data of this order is not generally available the method is extensively used by Martin in his study of London. Dot distribution maps, common in regional texts, may be usefully analysed in this way especially where no apparent concentration is visually discernible.

Methods of Measuring Concentration and Specialisation of Industries within and between regions

Generalised assumptions are often made about regional patterns of concentration, *e.g.* the woollen industry in Yorkshire or the pottery industry in Staffordshire, and it is valuable to ascertain such degrees of concentration in such a way that they may be readily compared. This may be achieved in one of three ways: by calculating the percentage of the nation's pottery employees in Staffordshire, by computing a location quotient or by determining the degree of specialisation. The percentage figure is the one most easily obtained but is of limited value because it is only looking at one particular industry whereas the other two indices reflect the general industrial structure of an area. Interpretation of the percentage figure is also difficult except where there is a marked degree of specialisation.

The location quotient may be determined by the formula below.

This method is helpful in that an index greater than one indicates the region has more than its share of that particular industry. A value of less than one that it has less than its share. The direct comparisons of such values can do much to correct assessments

$$\frac{\dfrac{\text{Number of people employed in Industry A in area X}}{\text{Number of people employed in all manufacturing industries in area X}}}{\dfrac{\text{Number of people employed nationally in Industry A}}{\text{Number of people employed nationally in all manufacturing industries}}}$$

made upon a visual inspection and also give a more positive answer than some percentage figures which may leave one undecided, *e.g.* 18% of a country's industry A is in area X.

The third way is to determine the degree of specialisation within a region using the formula:

Index of specialisation = $\sqrt{P_1^2 + P_2^2 \ldots P_n^2}$ where P_1 is the percentage of people employed in Industry 1. The worked examples are based upon tables contained in the *Department of Employment and Productivity Gazette*, together with local authority data, and may well elucidate the methodology.

Example 1. To determine the location quotient of shipbuilding in Scotland using the appropriate formula:

EXERCISE 2. Calculate location quotients for (*a*) the cotton industry and (*b*) the man-made fibre industry for each of the regions in Table 4.2. Compare the results and state the geographical implications of any differences noted.

EXERCISE 3. Evaluate statistically the degree of concentration of (*a*) the pottery industry and (*b*) the manufacture of motor vehicles.

Example 2. To determine the index of specialisation of industry within Herefordshire using the data contained in Table 4.3.

$$\text{Formula:} \quad \text{Index} = \sqrt{P_1^2 + P_2^2 \ldots P_n^2}$$
$$= \sqrt{12 \cdot 3^2 + 0 \cdot 2^2 \ldots 0 \cdot 3^2}$$
$$= \sqrt{849 \cdot 0}$$
$$= 29 \cdot 14.$$

$$\text{L.Q.} = \frac{\dfrac{\text{Number of people employed in shipbuilding in Scotland}}{\text{Number of people employed in all manufacturing industries in Scotland}}}{\dfrac{\text{Number of people employed in shipbuilding in Great Britain}}{\text{Number of people employed in all manufacturing industries in Great Britain}}} \quad \frac{\dfrac{48}{733}}{\dfrac{195}{8710}} = 2 \cdot 9.$$

Since the location quotient is greater than 1 it indicates that Scotland has more than its share of Great Britain's shipbuilding industry. To have a comparative value it is necessary to determine similar quotients for the other regions contained in Table 4.1.

EXERCISE 1. Determine which regions have more than their share of the shipbuilding industry of Great Britain.

The lower the index, the more diversified is the industrial structure of an area. How is it possible to decide whether or not the Herefordshire index is considered high or low? Evaluation can only come through comparison with other areas. Britton has calculated indices for sub-regions of the Bristol area a selection from which are: Bristol 31·4, Bridgwater 37·1, Bath 46·5, Chippenham 56·8.

TABLE 4.1

EMPLOYEES IN MANUFACTURING INDUSTRIES ANALYSED BY REGIONS

INDUSTRY	REGIONS										
	S.E.	E. Ang.	S.W.	W. Mids.	E. Mids.	Yorks. Humberside	N.W.	North	Scot.	Wales	G.B.
Food, drink, and tobacco	227	41	65	71	49	83	128	37	103	21	825
Chemicals and allied industries	170	11	13	27	19	46	117	55	33	26	517
Metal manufacturing	50	3	6	143	46	110	37	53	50	92	590
Engineering and electrical	849	56	110	309	149	168	314	123	184	58	2,320
Shipbuilding and marine engineering	41	3	18	1	1	8	31	42	48	2	195
Vehicles	251	16	60	204	53	44	116	11	40	20	815
Metal goods not elsewhere classified	129	4	12	208	22	70	61	14	25	23	568
Textiles	34	3	15	36	123	170	195	20	91	17	704
Leather, etc.	19	1	4	6	4	6	9	2	4	2	57
Clothing and footwear	139	14	25	23	75	56	88	34	31	15	500
Bricks and pottery, etc.	87	8	11	83	24	36	47	19	24	11	350
Timber and furniture	122	11	19	24	18	27	34	15	25	7	302
Paper, printing, and publishing	304	17	37	33	26	40	90	17	58	12	634
Others	125	7	16	47	17	12	60	17	17	15	333
Totals	2,547	195	411	1,215	626	876	1,327	459	733	321	8,710

TABLE 4.2

EMPLOYEES IN SELECTED SUB-SECTIONAL MANUFACTURING INDUSTRIES ANALYSED BY REGIONS

INDUSTRY	REGIONS										
	S.E.	E. Ang	S.W.	W. Mids.	E. Hum-berside	Yorks. Hum-berside	N.W.	North	Scot.	Wales	G.B.
Motor vehicle manufacture	155	14	13	160	8	22	61	5	19	13	470
Man-made fibres	—	—	3	6	5	7	6	3	—	10	40
Cotton	2	—	—	3	5	9	53	1	4	—	77
Woollens	2	—	4	1	4	116	9	6	18	—	160
Men's and boys' tailored wear ..	20	2	3	7	6	36	12	16	9	5	116
Pottery	3	—	1	51	2	—	2	—	—	—	59

Notes on Tables 4.1 *and* 4.2.

Source of data: Department of Employment and Productivity Gazette, April, 1968.

Numbers are estimated numbers in thousands and have been rounded up to the nearest thousand.

Industries in Table 4.1 are those of the minimum list headings of the Standard Industrial Classification, whilst those in Table 4.2 are sub-sections of these, *e.g.* Motor vehicle manufacture (4.2) is a sub-division of Vehicles in Table 4.1.

Where no figure is given this may indicate either that no one is employed in this particular industry or that no figure is available.

EXERCISE. Determine the indices of specialisation for Wales and the south-east (Table 4.1). To what extent do they exemplify those characteristics you associated with a development area and an affluent society respectively?

Activity Rates

Activity rates which are often quoted in the regional

TABLE 4.3

INSURED POPULATION—HEREFORDSHIRE, JUNE, 1966.

S.I.C. Order No.	Males	Females	Total	Percentage
1	4,505	910	5,415	12·3
2	102	2	104	0·2
3	1,809	1,572	3,381	7·7
4	34	—	34	0·1
5	3,052	307	3,359	7·6
6	1,452	699	2,151	4·9
7	—	—	—	—
8	570	230	800	1·8
9	231	195	426	1·0
10	72	19	91	0·2
11	47	7	54	0·1
12	7	195	202	0·5
13	519	167	686	1·6
14	408	62	470	1·1
15	372	215	587	1·3
16	366	200	566	1·2
17	3,199	152	3,351	7·6
18	691	76	767	1·7
19	1,692	412	2,113	4·8
20	2,340	2,931	5,271	11·9
21	453	313	766	1·7
22	1,447	3,940	5,387	12·2
23	1,904	2,607	4,511	10·2
24	2,468	1,044	3,512	8·0
25	101	47	148	0·3
Totals	27,841	16,311	44,311	100·0

Source: Unpublished local Department of Employment and Productivity Records.

plans of the Department of Economic Affairs, *e.g.* the West Midlands study, express the relationship between the number of people employed and the number of people of working age, and hence who in theory provide employment potential. Low activity rates have sometimes been regarded as evidence of concealed unemployment, but in fact, they may reflect the sociological trends or particular industrial structures of an area. A low index, whilst indicating that a potential labour force may exist, does not in itself offer any guarantee that such potential will be realised: a more satisfactory guide is the number registered as unemployed.

TABLE 4.4. POPULATION FIGURES FOR HEREFORDSHIRE

Source: County Census Report.

Males of all ages ..	64,605	Males aged 15–65 ..	41,662
Females of all ages ..	66,323	Females aged 15–60 ..	37,305
Totals ..	130,928	Totals ..	78,967

The activity rate is obtained by using the formula:

$$\text{Activity Rate} = \frac{\text{Number employed} \times 100}{\text{Total population of working age}}$$

Indices may be obtained for males and females as well as for total populations and those for Herefordshire using Tables 4.3 and 4.4 are

Male $\dfrac{27,841}{41,662} \times 100 = 66\cdot8.$

Female $\dfrac{16,311}{37,305} \times 100 = 43\cdot7.$

Total $\dfrac{44,311}{78,967} \times 100 = 56\cdot1.$

It is reasonable to expect a lower activity rate for women than for men in our society, but would the difference be as great in a Yorkshire textile town as is indicated for this rural county? National customs too vary and in the U.S.S.R. it may be assumed that the female activity rate would closely approximate to that of the male. Again these indices have more meaning when compared with those for other regions: some quoted by Britton include Bristol 57·6, Chippenham 47·3, Bridgwater 52·0, Bath 42·8, and Taunton 45·8. The figures for Herefordshire would seem to be comparatively high and the question may be asked why it is not of the same order as that for Taunton with which it has other common features.

Geographical Relationships

It has always been possible to make qualitative statements about the relationship of one group of activities with another, e.g. from Table 4.2 it may be deduced there is a connection between the distribution in the manufacture of woollens and that of the men's tailored wear industry, partially because of the traditional association of the ready-made clothing industry with Yorkshire, supported by the high employment figures in both these industries in the region. The 20,000 employed in tailored wear in the south-east cannot be ignored and might be explained away by reference to the fashion houses of London. Further analysis through conventional methods is thereafter defied.

Correlation indices which show degrees of association and possibly dependence of one industry with another enable the geographer to make a quantitative statement. The simplest method to employ is that of the Spearman Rank correlation coefficient, full instructions for which, together with a worked example, appear in Chapter 6. Only a brief synopsis is therefore included below.

The closeness of association is revealed by the proximity of the index to 1; this is established by measuring the difference in rank order of the two phenomena and substituting in a formula, e.g. the rank order for the woollen industry in Table 4.2 is: 1 Yorkshire and Humberside, 2 Scotland, 3 Northwest, 4 North, 5·5 South-west and East Midlands, 7 South-east, 8 West Midlands, and 9·5 East Anglia and Wales. Where two numbers tie, as in the case of the south-west and east Midlands, then the mean rank order of the two is allocated to each. To complete the computation it is necessary to establish the rank order of men's tailored wear, determine the deviation and apply the formula. The result in this case gives an index of 0·33 (to two significant figures) and is not statistically significant (see Chap. 6).

However, this low correlation index necessitates a re-assessment of the pre-conceived idea of association, and from it may be deduced that the tailoring industry is by no means closely related to its supply of raw materials. To establish whether or not the industry is market orientated, a similar procedure is necessary comparing the regional distribution of the clothing industry with that of population. Many sets of phenomena may all be compared with each other with the aid of a computer and all the inter-relationships expressed in a correlation matrix, examples of which may be found in Martin's study of the industries of Greater London.

EXERCISE. Measure the degree of association between motor vehicle manufacturing and the engineering and electrical engineering industries. To what extent does this confirm the view that the motor car industry is dependent upon components being near at hand? Data for this exercise may be found in Tables 4.1 and 4.2 and detailed instructions in Chapter 6, p. 54.

Conclusion

Some attempt has been made to emphasise the complexity of industrial location patterns and to caution the geographer against simple explanations in terms of material resources. It is hoped that some appreciation of the chance element operating within an environmental framework will have been gained from the simulation exercise. The simple methodology of data processing has been introduced but it must be understood that only when a data bank of comparative indices has been established, will direct comparisons of a quantitative nature become effective.

QUESTIONNAIRE FOR INVESTIGATION OF INDUSTRY

Name of Firm

Address

Location of Factory

1. Why is the factory located on its present site?
2. When was the factory built on this site?
3. Is this the original site?
4. If not the original site, please give details of its location and indicate reasons for moving.
5. What are the specific advantages of your present site compared with alternatives in Herefordshire in particular or Britain in particular? Are there any disadvantages?

Advantages

Disadvantages

Products of the Factory

1. Please list in order of importance all the finished products made in your factory, giving approximate indications of scale where possible.
2. Are any of these products used as raw materials in another factory? Please give details of location.
3. Do you carry out any part processing?
4. What changes of type and importance of product have been made during the past five years?

Market Area

1. List major towns to which finished products are sent—
   (*a*) in U.K.   (*b*) Overseas.

United Kingdom

Overseas

2. Indicate what percentage of your market is (*a*) local, (*b*) national, (*c*) international.
3. To what extent has the market changed in size or location during the last five years?
4. Do you anticipate any major change in either trend or location in the next five years? Please give reasons if possible.
5. What media do you use to advertise your products and to what extent do you think they are really effective?

Raw Materials Used

Please list in the table below in order of significance all the raw materials used indicating where possible individual weights and showing place of origin.

RAW MATERIAL	WEIGHT	PLACE OF ORIGIN

Are any raw materials in semi-processed form? Please give details.

Labour

1. Total number employed.
2. Total number of men employed........ women employed.....
3. Total numbers of skilled.... semi-skilled.... unskilled.....
4. What changes in the structure of this labour force have been effected during the past five years particularly as a result of new machinery and/or improved techniques?
5. What are your minimal entrance requirements for employees?
6. How long is the training period for your employees?
7. Do you have formal apprenticeship schemes?
8. Is all your labour force recruited locally? If not, from where do you recruit them?

Transport

1. What means of transport do you use for—
   (*a*) bringing in raw materials?
   (*b*) marketing finished products?

2. What are the advantages of the method you use compared with alternative forms of transport?
3. Does either the weight, bulk, or fragility of your materials and products pose any special transport problems?
4. If you export abroad, which port do you use and why this particular one?

Power

What form of power do you use and where does it come from?

Water

Do you use water in very large quantities? Where does the water you use come from?

Organisation

1. Is your factory part of a chain or group of factories either in this area or the U.K.? If so, what specific part does your particular plant play? What is the location of the parent factory and of other subsidiaries?
2. Is your factory fully integrated or does it depend heavily upon the products of other factories?
3. What do you consider to be the advantages and/or disadvantages of being located in a predominately rural/urban area.
   Advantages
   Disadvantages
   Any further comment you wish to make

SUGGESTIONS FOR FURTHER READING FOR CHAPTERS 3 AND 4

1. Alexander, J. W. *Economic Geography* (Part nine), Prentice Hall, New Jersey, 1963.
2. Alexandersson, G. *Geography of Manufacturing*, Prentice Hall, New Jersey, 1967.
3. Britton, J. N. H. *Regional Analysis and Economic Geography*, Bell, London, 1967. A case study of manufacturing in the Bristol region.
4. Chisholm, M. *Geography and Economics*, Bell, London, 1966.
5. Estall, R. C. *New England: A Study in Industrial Adjustment*, Bell, London, 1966.
6. Estall, R. C., and Buchanan, R. O. *Industrial Activity and Economic Geography*, Hutchinson, London, 1961.
7. Hall, P. "Grids for Geographers." *New Society*, October 12th, 1967.
8. Hamilton, F. E. I. "Models of Industrial Geography" (Chap. 10 of *Socio-economic Models in Geography*, ed. Chorley & Haggett), Methuen, London, 1968.
9. Harris, Chauncy D. "The Market as a Factor in the Localisation of Industry in the United States." *A.A.A.G*, Vol. 44, 1954.
10. Keeble, D. "School Teaching and Urban Geography: Some New Approaches", *Geography*, **54**, 1969, 18 (contains elaboration of the simulation technique).
11. Martin, J. E. *Greater London, an Industrial Geography*, Bell, London, 1966.

Reproduced by permission of John Bartholomew & Son

QUARTER-INCH MAP

Taunton District

Part of Sheet 16

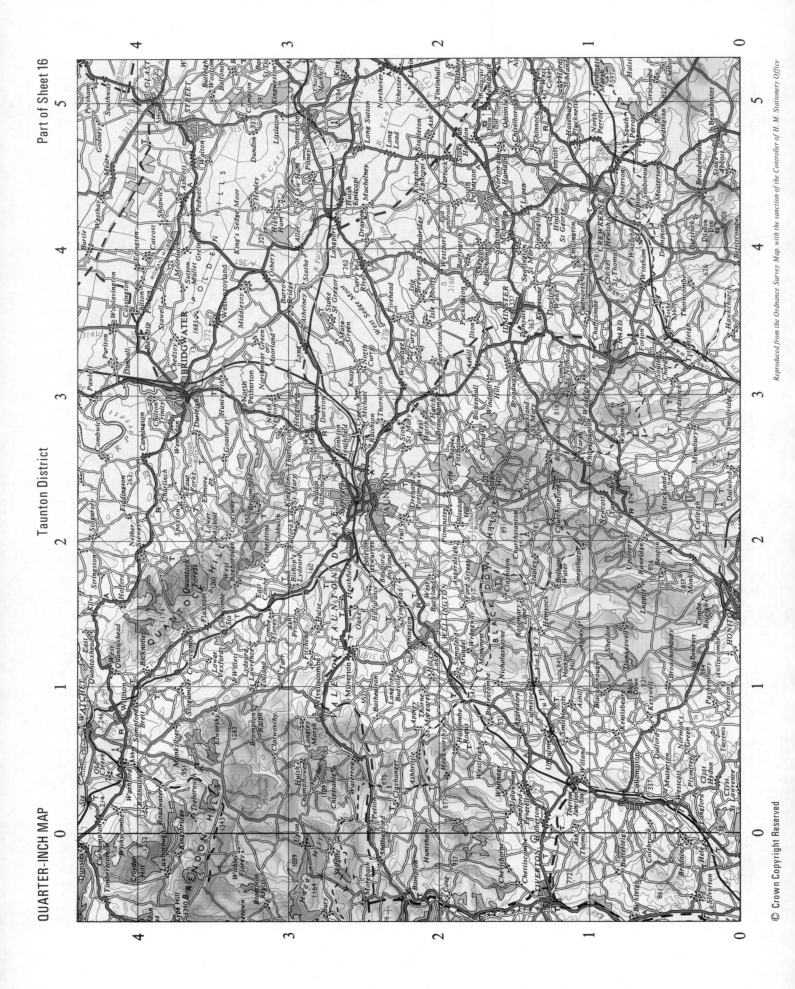

12. McCarty, H. H. and Linberg, J. B. *A Preface to Economic Geography*, Prentice Hall, New Jersey, 1966.

13. Pounds, N. J. G. *The Geography of Iron and Steel*, Hutchinson, London, 1959.

14. Smith, W. *The Location of Industry*. Transactions I.B.G., **21**, 1955.

15. Watson, W. "Uneconomic Geography", Editorial in *Economic Geography*, **43**, 1967.

16. *The West Midlands*. H.M.S.O. Department of Economic Affairs.

STANDARD OCCUPATION ORDERS AND STANDARD INDUSTRIAL CLASSIFICATION

STANDARD INDUSTRIAL CLASSIFICATION ORDERS

I. Agriculture Forestry, Fishing.
II. Mining and Quarrying.
III. Food, Drink, and Tobacco.
IV. Chemicals and Allied Industries.
V. Metal Manufacture.
VI. Engineering and Electrical Goods.
VII. Shipbuilding and Marine Engineering.
VIII. Vehicles.
IX. Metal Goods (N.E.S.).
X. Textiles.
XI. Leather, Leather Goods, and Fur.
XII. Clothing and Footwear.
XIII. Bricks, Pottery, Glass, Cement.
XIV. Timber and Furniture.
XV. Paper, Printing, and Publishing.
XVI. Other Manufacturing Industries (Rubber, Toys, Plastics).
XVII. Construction.
XVIII. Gas, Electricity, and Water.
XIX. Transport and Communication.
XX. Distributive Trades.
XXI. Insurance, Banking and Finance.
XXII. Professional and Scientific Services.
XXIII. Miscellaneous Services (Catering, Laundries, Hairdressing, Motor repairs).
XXIV. Public Administration and Defence.

N.E.S.—Not elsewhere specified.

Note.—Only the orders are given, minimum list headings, *e.g.*

Order V. Metal Manufacture.
311 Iron and Steel.
312 Steel Tubes.
313 Iron Castings.
321 Light Metals.
322 Copper, Brass, and other base metals.

Source: Standard Industrial Classification, H.M.S.O.

OCCUPATION ORDERS

I. Farmers, Foresters, Fishermen.
II. Miners and Quarrymen.
III. Gas, Coke and, Chemical Makers.
IV. Glass and Ceramic Makers.
V. Furnace, Forge, Foundry, and Rolling Mill Workers.
VI. Electrical and Electronic Workers.
VII. Engineering and Allied Trade Workers.
VIII. Woodworkers.
IX. Leather Workers.
X. Textile Workers.
XI. Clothing Workers.
XII. Food, Drink, and Tobacco Workers.
XIII. Paper and Printing Workers.
XIV. Makers of Other Products (Rubber and Plastics).
XV. Construction Workers.
XVI. Painters and Decorators.
XVII. Drivers of Stationary Engines and Cranes.
XVIII. Labourers (N.E.C.).
XIX. Transport and Communication Workers.
XX. Warehousemen, Storekeepers, Packers, and Bottlers.
XXI. Clerical Workers.
XXII. Sales Workers.
XXIII. Service, Sport, and Recreation Workers.

XXIV. Administrators and Managers.
XXV. Professional, Technical, Artists.
XXVI. Armed Forces.
XXVII. Inadequately described Occupations.

N.E.C.—Not elsewhere classified.

Each order is broken down into—
Order XII. Food, Drink, Tobacco.
080 Bakers and Pastry Cooks.
081 Butchers and Meat Cutters.
082 Brewers and Wine Makers.
083 Food Processors N.E.C.

CHAPTER 5

SETTLEMENT PATTERNS

Introduction. Distribution: Nearest Neighbour Analysis; Distribution and Size. Central Place Theory. Rank Size. Methods of Delimiting Spheres of Influence. 1. The Town Function as a Base. 2. The Countryside as a Base. 3. The Relative Attraction of Towns within an Area.

Introduction

The settlement pattern to be found in any area is perhaps the ultimate expression of man in space and it is not therefore surprising that the arrangement should be complex. Such patterns are evolving through all times and that of Iron Age Britain compared with to-day's arrangement has been inverted. Similar in contrast is the market town pattern associated with an essentially rural community compared with the clustered agglomerations resulting from the industrial revolution. The contemporary expression is that of the deliberately planned town in

There is essentially a duality in the study of settlements, (*a*) spatial distributions, numbers and sizes, and their inter-relationships, and (*b*) the morphology and function of individual units. It is these two aspects which will be considered in turn in this and the subsequent chapter.

Distribution

1. *Distribution.*—The arrangement of settlements on the Somerset and Lincolnshire map extracts are shown in Fig. 5.3 (*a*) and (*b*), and any attempt to describe accurately or to analyse purposefully these

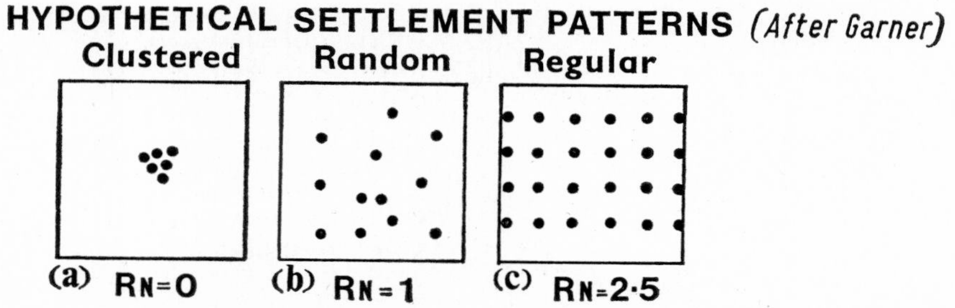

FIG. 5.1. Hypothetical settlement patterns. Rn values indicate degree of randomness. (See Fig. 5.4.)

a planned location, *e.g.* Harlow or Dawley—the so-called "New Towns". The time element, then, is one of the factors complicating any understanding or rationalisation of the present scene.

Emphasis in the past has been given to the important role of physical factors affecting the siting of settlements such as spring lines, gaps, and defensive knolls. Whilst abundant evidence of these can be found, there are equally many sites in non-descript situations which could not be explained by physical factors. Upon close examination of either map or ground one often asks, "why here and not there" (though physical factors are identical) and so we come to perhaps the strongest single element underlying settlement patterns—that of the chance or rational decision of man.

patterns presents difficulties. Three tentative categories are usually suggested:

(1) *Uniform or regular* where ideally each settlement is equidistant from its six nearest neighbours. Often this pattern is distorted when a competitive element precludes the presence of a similar settlement close by. This is particularly evident in the spacing of market towns in rural areas such as East Anglia. However, given certain idealised conditions the arrangement of such market towns should be hexagonal as in the theory of Christaller to be discussed later in this chapter.

(2) *Clustered.*—A marked grouping of settlements may take place as on the coalfields of England or in the textile or pottery regions.

(3) *Random.*—Settlements may well appear to be distributed in a random manner such as the villages of the Somerset countryside shown in Fig. 5.3 (*b*).

Clearly any classification into the above groups is limited both to the historical time and the study area within which it is made. What appears as random in a small area may appear clustered when the study area is greatly enlarged, *e.g.* the woollen towns of the West Riding would appear differently in a map of the

Nearest Neighbour Analysis

To describe a settlement pattern such as that depicted in Fig. 5.3 (*b*) merely using visual methods would at best be subjective and dependent upon the individual observer. Two people may see different faces in the embers of the same fire. Nearest neighbour analysis enables one to give a quantitative and scientific description of the pattern; it is possible to

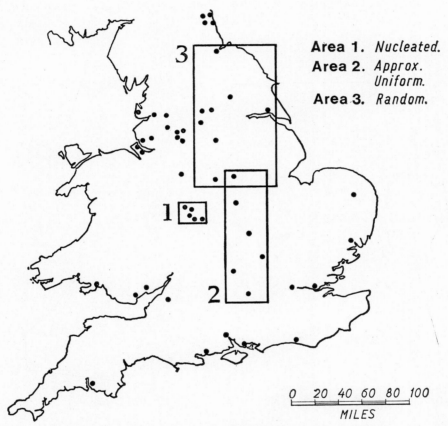

Area 1. *Nucleated.*
Area 2. *Approx. Uniform.*
Area 3. *Random.*

FIG. 5.2. Map showing distribution of towns in England and Wales with a population greater than 100,000.
Note: 22 London Boroughs in this category are generalised into one dot.

Riding alone than in maps of Yorkshire or northern England as a whole.

The three major categories of clustered, uniform or regular, and random are shown in abstract form in Fig. 5.1 and with an example from the real world in Fig. 5.2. The category of a given settlement pattern may be determined by the method of nearest neighbour analysis which is now described and illustrated with a worked example.

measure the degree of randomness and to determine the extent of deviation from randomness. This is obtained from the scale as shown in Fig. 5.4. This RN scale gives a comparative measurement between areas as well as within them. There are three important values on the scale: 1·0 indicating a completely random distribution, 0 indicating absolute clustering and, at the other extreme 2·1491 indicating an entirely dispersed pattern.

Procedure for Nearest Neighbour Analysis

The basic technique is that used for a long time by plant ecologists to measure and record the distance separating one object from its nearest neighbour.

(1) Reduce the distribution to a series of dots as shown in Fig. 5.3 (*a*). The criteria for selecting the dots are dependent upon the individual use of the map, *e.g.* one may choose all settlements within the area or all settlements within a certain population range, *e.g.* 500-1,000. In any event, one needs a minimum of thirty dots from which to measure if the

bours may be outside the study area. It is, however, in order to measure to these peripheral dots from others within the area. Join all the peripheral dots to form a "buffer zone", *i.e.* points Nos. 37-59 of Fig. 5.3 (*a*).

(3) Number all the dots on the map and from each in turn measure and record the distance to its nearest neighbour as shown in Fig. 5.5. Note all measurements are to the point's nearest neighbour and it is possible to measure back to the previous point when relevant, as is the case in point 2 in Fig. 5.5. Table

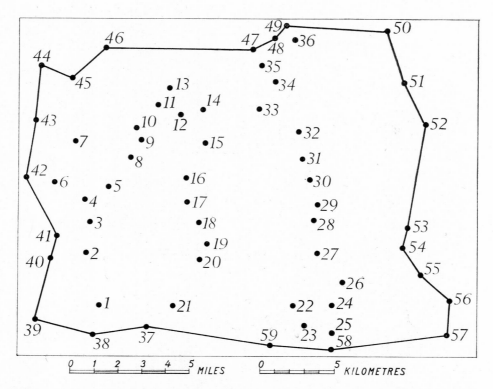

FIG. 5.3 (*a*). Nearest neighbour analysis: settlement pattern in a part of Lincolnshire. (For explanation see text and Map 1.)

result is to have real validity. In the examples given all the settlements with a church were reduced to a dot to form Fig. 5.3 (*a*), whilst all named settlements other than farms in the Somerset extract form the basis for Fig. 5.3 (*b*). These diagrams have all the limitations of a dot distribution map, but since we are concerned with relative locations rather than absolute ones, the generalisation of the dot is not particularly significant.

(2) The dots on the boundary may not be used as bases of measurement because their nearest neigh-

5.1 records the measurements for Fig. 5.5 whilst full details for Fig. 5.3 (*a*) are given in Table 5.2.

TABLE 5.1.

Point No. 1 Distance to nearest neighbour	1 in.
2	1 in.
3	2 in.

(4) Add all the distances and divide by the number of measurements taken to obtain the mean. This is known as the observed or measured mean and in the worked example for Lincolnshire is 35·9 ÷ 36 = 0·99.

(5) Determine the density of points in the area by the formula

$$\text{Density} = \frac{\text{Number of points in study area}}{\text{Area of study area}}$$

Expected Mean =

$$\frac{1}{2 \sqrt{\text{Density}}} = \frac{1}{2 \sqrt{0 \cdot 225}} = \frac{1}{0 \cdot 95} = 1 \cdot 1.$$

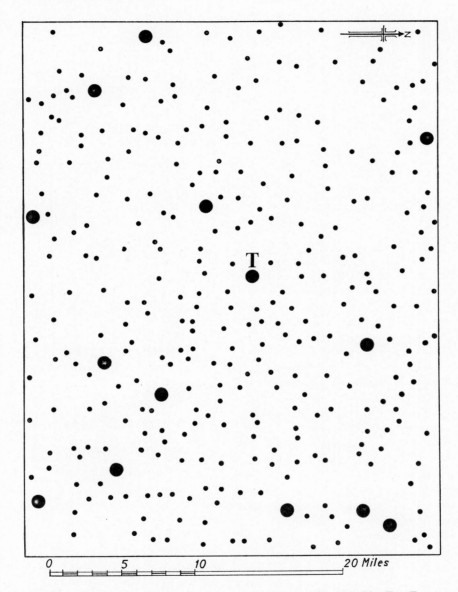

FIG. 5.3 (b). Settlement pattern of an area of Somerset. (See Map 2.) T = Taunton.

The units of area should be the same as those used for measuring distances, *i.e.* miles, and for the worked example the density is

$$\frac{59 \text{ (Total number of points)}}{262 \cdot 7 \text{ (Area in square miles)}} = 0 \cdot 225.$$

(6) Calculate the expected mean in a random distribution by the formula

(7) Finally, determine the random scale value by the formula

Degree of randomness =

$$\frac{\text{Observed or measured mean}}{\text{Expected mean in a random distribution}}$$

$$R_N = \frac{0 \cdot 99}{1 \cdot 1} = 0 \cdot 9.$$

TABLE 5.2

Point No. from which measurement is taken	Distance in miles to nearest neighbour	Point No. from which measurement is taken	Distance in miles to nearest neighbour	Point No. from which measurement is taken	Distance in miles to nearest neighbour
1	1·0	13	0·8	25	1·1
2	1·1	14	0·8	26	1·9
3	1·2	15	1·2	27	1·2
4	0·8	16	1·0	28	0·8
5	0·8	17	1·0	29	0·8
6	1·0	18	0·6	30	0·7
7	1·8	19	0·6	31	0·7
8	1·0	20	0·9	32	1·3
9	0·7	21	1·5	33	1·4
10	0·7	22	0·9	34	1·0
11	0·9	23	0·9	35	0·6
12	0·8	24	1·2	36	1·2

Note.—No measurements are made from points Nos. 37–59 because they are on the periphery.

Total number of measurements taken is 36.

Subjectively one would judge the pattern in Fig. 5.3 (*a*) to be linear clustered, especially as it is this which is normally associated with a limestone upland adjacent to a fenland area. Thus the RN value of 0·9 approximating to a random distribution is surprising and one may increase the size of the study area to see if this has materially and significantly affected the result. (Readers may recall this was mentioned earlier as a limitation of this technique.) Alternatively, one may seek more diligently for reasons why such a deviation from the expected result should have occurred. For comparative purposes it is interesting to note that a sample area based on Taunton [Fig. 5.3 (*b*)] yielded a value of 1·2. Visually it would have been difficult to compare these two patterns yet here we have a direct comparison in statistical terms revealing a much closer relationship than one would have deduced from usual mapwork. Patterns in contrasting economic regions such as a coalfield and adjacent rural area may prove rewarding, but in this instance the standardisation of size in selecting settlements would be a wise precaution if any valid deduction is to be made. This technique may be applied to any dot distribution map, frequently found in economic geography, provided one realises the innate limitations of such maps and the technique themselves.

Operational note when a large number of points is involved.

1. Number the points as before and eliminate the peripheral ones.

2. Call random numbers (using the table printed on p. 79, and following the instructions for their use) to give a sample of 30 dots from which to measure to their nearest neighbour.

(3) Proceed as before.

EXERCISE. To test the hypothesis that little difference exists between the settlement pattern around Taunton and that around Hereford in view of the similarity of physical landscape and type of rural economy common to both areas.

Method.—Calculate the RN value for rural settlement for the area on Map 2 (Somerset) which lies

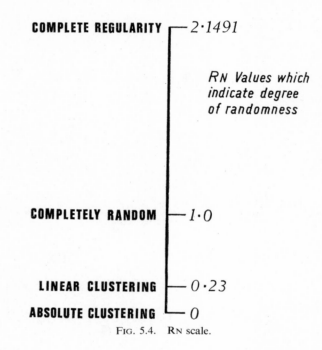

COMPLETE REGULARITY — 2·1491

RN Values which indicate degree of randomness

COMPLETELY RANDOM — 1·0

LINEAR CLUSTERING — 0·23

ABSOLUTE CLUSTERING — 0

FIG. 5.4. RN scale.

north and east of the Grid Lines 2 and 2. Calculate the RN value for the area on Map 3 (Herefordshire) north of grid line 4 and bounded in the west by grid line 3 and in the east by grid line 6. Proceed according to the worked example provided for the Lincoln area.

Distribution and Size

Settlements of varying size exist throughout the world and it is vitally important for geography defined as a "science concerned with the rational development and testing of theories that explain and predict the spatial distribution and location of various characteristics on the surface of the earth" (Yeates) to determine whether there is any order or pattern in their size and spacing. The main hypotheses to be tested here are: (1) As settlements increase in size so they become fewer in number and (2) As settlements increase in size so the distance separating them also increases. The tables below help to provide statistical evidence to support these hypotheses. Table 5.3 (*a*) summarises the findings of Christaller's work in Southern Germany, Table 5.3 (*b*) that of Berry's work in Saskatchewan, whilst the impact of industry is revealed in Table 5.3 (*c*). Figures for part of the county of Somerset shown in Table 5.3 (*d*) indicate that it is quite possible to test the theory on a smaller scale and in a less sophisticated manner merely by using an O.S. map.

TABLE 5.3 (*a*)

CHRISTALLER'S TOWN GROUPINGS IN SOUTHERN GERMANY

Central Place	Approximate Population	Distance Apart (in miles)	Service Area (sq. miles)
Market Hamlet	1,000	4·5	18
Township centre	2,000	7·5	54
County seat	4,000	13·0	160
District city	10,000	22·5	480
Small state capital	30,000	39·0	1,500
Provincial head city	100,000	67·5	4,500
Regional capital city	500,000	116·0	13,500

Source: Rutherford Logan and Missen, *New Viewpoints in Economic Geography*, p. 372.

TABLE 5.3 (*b*)

CHARACTERISTICS OF CENTRES IN SASKATCHEWAN, 1961

Classification	Number	Average Spacing (in miles)
Hamlet	404	9·6
Village	150	13·5
Town	100	19·8
Small seat	85	22·5
County seat	29	39·5
Regional city	9	67·5
Regional capital	2	144·0

Source: Berry, *Geography of Market Centres and Retail Distribution*, p. 116.

TABLE 5.3 (*c*)

TOWN SPACING IN AN INDUSTRIAL REGION OF ENGLAND AND WALES.

Mean Spacing of Medium Sized Towns in Miles
20,000— 30,000 inhabitants 6·1
40,000— 50,000 inhabitants 7·9
75,000—100,000 inhabitants 10·0

Source: Haggett, *Locational Analysis in Human Geography*, p. 109.

The figures in Table 5.3 (*c*) should be compared with those of Table 5.3 (*a*) to see the impact of industry upon the hitherto rural landscape.

TABLE 5.3 (*d*)

SPACING OF SETTLEMENTS ON THE SOMERSET EXTRACT MAP

Number of		Mean Distance Apart
Hamlet/village approx.	298	1·1 miles
Towns below 10,000,	9	6·9 miles
Towns 10,000–30,000,	2	26·0 miles
Towns over 30,000,	1	

Table 5.3 (*d*) could be improved by using the county census and categorising all the settlements in the county, but it is included as an example of what may be done in school in a very limited time and with limited resources.

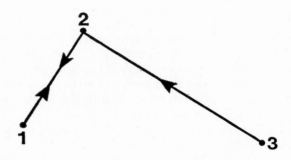

Arrows indicate direction of measurement

FIG. 5.5. Nearest neighbour analysis.

EXERCISE. With reference to Fig. 5.2 determine the mean distance separating the towns shown by measuring the distance of each town from its nearest neighbour and dividing the total distance by the number of measurements. How does this distance compare with that of the corresponding town category in Table 5.3 (*a*)?

Central Place Theory

A convenient starting point for any analysis of the relationship between spacing and size of settlements is the work of Christaller and Losch who, despite the apparently abstract nature of their theses, provide a framework for study.

The essence of Christaller's theory is that a certain amount of productive land supports an urban unit which performs essential services for that land. These services performed purely for a surrounding area are called central functions and the settlements performing them, central places, hence the name central place theory. Ideally each central place should have a circular tributary area as may be seen in Fig. 5.6 (*a*) and (*b*). Since circles would either overlap or leave areas unserved the best theoretical shape is that of the

the central place concept to be evident, should it have validity at the present time. There is then more empirical evidence for Christaller's theory in reality

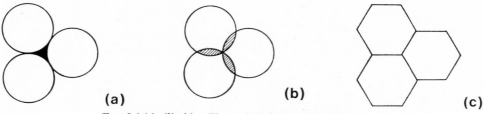

Fig. 5.6 (*a*), (*b*), (*c*).   Theoretical shapes of trading areas.

hexagon as shown in Fig. 5.6 (*c*).

As shown in Fig. 5.7 a hierarchy of centres emerges *i.e.* a large number of villages each serving small areas, a smaller number of towns serving larger areas, and one city serving a very large area. This is apparent in Table 5.3 (*a*) emphasising the relationship between size and spacing of settlements. Notice for any given level in the hierarchy all centres are equidistant from each other.

The premises upon which Christaller based his theory were not dissimilar to those of von Thunen (Chap. 3) namely:

(1) Distribution of population and purchasing power should be uniform.

(2) Physical characteristics and resources should be uniform.

(3) Transport facilities in all directions should be equal.

Clearly in the real world these premises cannot readily be met and distortions of the triangular lattice are frequently caused by variations in relief, differences in transport media and densities (the world becomes ever more mobile), presence of mineral resources and industrial development. Critics of Christaller have complained of the rigidity of his arrangement and of its abstract nature, yet it must be remembered that the theory was developed in the essentially agrarian society of Southern Germany, whereas we live in a predominantly industrial one. It is interesting to note the spacing of market towns in East Anglia shows a reasonable approximation to a regular lattice as do those of Herefordshire (Map 3) and to a lesser extent those of Somerset (Map 2). These are largely rural areas, where one would expect

than might at first appear, although the discovery of the hexagonal network is extremely difficult due in large measure to the complexities of the modern

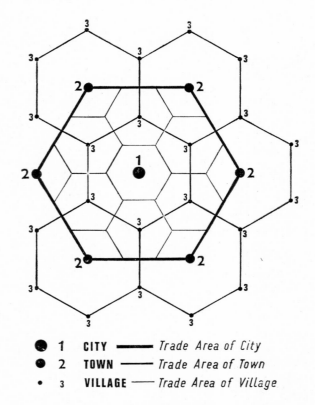

●	1	CITY	—— *Trade Area of City*
●	2	TOWN	—— *Trade Area of Town*
·	3	VILLAGE	—— *Trade Area of Village*

Fig. 5.7.   Hierarchy of central places and their trading areas. (Based on Alexander: *Economic Geography*.)

world and the functional changes affecting settlement on the contemporary scene. These are elaborated in the next section.

EXERCISE 1. Construct a frequency histogram indicating the number of contact sides for each county of England and Wales. This is determined by the number of counties which surround any one county. How does this compare with a similar histogram for the states of the U.S.A.? In either case, is there any evidence to support a hexagonal arrangement of states or counties?

EXERCISE 2. Measure the mean distance separating the market towns on Maps 2 and 3. How does this compare with the distance separating towns of a similar order in Table 5.2 (*a*)? Comment upon the reasons for any similarity or difference you note.

Why Christaller's Theory breaks down in the real world.

Perhaps the prime reason for discrepancies between Christaller's theory and reality on the present scene may be identified as changes in type of economy, transport media, and town functions between then and now. In addition, like von Thünen, he deliberately excluded variables, such as relief, from his thesis. Reasons may therefore be listed as:

(1) The topography of a region is rarely uniform.

(2) Resources are not uniformly distributed.

(3) As a result of the two previous factors the distribution of population and the provision of transport facilities is not even.

(4) Means of transport in differing periods of historical time affect the degree of mobility of people and hence the location of their settlements.

(5) Whereas Christaller considered settlements as having only a central place function, in modern society this is not necessarily their primary *raison d'être*. Although it may still not be the dominant one, towns may develop this function at a later stage.

The reasons for urban growth are written about substantially in the literature on urban geography and it will suffice here merely to list some of the reasons for the location and growth of towns in the contemporary world:

(*a*) Physical resources such as minerals may generate a clustering.

(*b*) Break of bulk points on or between transport routes and media often occur in coastal or valley locations thus generating linear arrangements.

(*c*) Industrial towns tend to congregate together to achieve scale economies, *e.g.* textile or pottery towns in the B.I.

(*d*) Leisure towns are frequently found along the coast.

(*e*) Planned towns to diversify the economy may be sited largely for social reasons.

Rank Size

Permeating the whole of the theory of the spacing of settlements is the concept of a hierarchy. Each central place has a number of smaller places dependent upon it. In modern society the range of a "good", *i.e.* the distance people travel to obtain a particular function, and the "threshold", *i.e.* the minimum number of people required to support a particular function, perpetuate this hierarchical arrangement, for the ability of a settlement to maintain a specific range of good and threshold will depend upon its size. This theme will be elaborated in Chapter 6 which is concerned with individual settlements and their functions.

We have seen that as the size of settlements increases so their number decreases and this has led to the rank size hypothesis: For any given region there will be a primate city and all other city sizes will be related to that of this primate city. This relationship expressed by the formula $P_N = P_1(N)^{-1}$, simply means that the second city in the region should be half the size of the first, the third one-third of its size, and so the ratio continues. A necessary preliminary to test this hypothesis is to rank all the cities and/or towns in the study area. The plotting of the rank size rule can be seen in graph form in Fig. 5.8 where (*a*) is the postulated case, (*b*) the urban areas for England and Wales in 1961, and (*c*) the fifteen highest ranking towns in the county of Hampshire.

Testing the Rank Size Rule

The relationship between the first and second largest cities for seventy-two different countries has been tested by Stewart who found that on average the primate city was three and a quarter times the size of the next city rather than the twice suggested by the rule. Using the population statistics found in Phillips *Geographical Digest*, it is an easy exercise to test this relationship since the towns are arranged in rank order. Graphs showing the application of rank size rule to the whole range of urban settlements show that the U.S.A. conforms closely to the rule whilst Australia diverges strongly from it. These again may be plotted and tested, using the data obtained from the Phillips Digest. It has been suggested that figures for an entire area such as a country seem to conform rather better than those for part of an area such as a county or state and this is clearly indicated in Fig. 5.8 where the graph for the national area shows a closer approximation to the rank size rule than does that for the single county.

From the work of Berry, who analysed thirty-eight countries, certain tentative generalisations have been made to help form an ordered structure. Approximations to rank size distribution are found in the

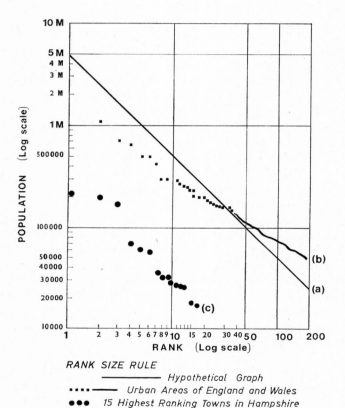

RANK SIZE RULE
———— Hypothetical Graph
■■■■■——— Urban Areas of England and Wales
●●● 15 Highest Ranking Towns in Hampshire

FIG. 5.8.   The rank size rule.

larger countries which are economically advanced and have a long tradition of urban growth whilst the greatest divergence is found in predominantly agrarian countries with a large number of small towns. Care should be taken in making any generalisation, however, since the U.S.A., Korea, China, and El Salvador all approximate to the rank size rule despite differences in area, population density, and type of economy. Whatever its limitations the rank size rule does substantiate the theory of Christaller, as do varied pieces of

empirical evidence of a definite hierarchical structure to settlement patterns (as shown in the tables contained in this chapter). This further emphasises the inseparable relationship between size, number, and spacing as postulated at the beginning of this section.

EXERCISE 1.   A simple exercise can be worked for Argentina or indeed any country where the only data necessary is a school atlas and the population figures for the major towns obtainable from any standard regional textbook. In testing the rank size rule in Argentina it will be found that the figures for Rosario and Cordoba, the second and third cities, are 1/11 and 1/12 respectively. This is quite unlike the usual pattern and the distortion is due to the enormous size and dominance of Buenos Aires in the country. This easily calculated relationship shows in an objective way the dominance of the capital and could be compared with adjacent Latin American countries or an Australian State. Another way in which the dominance of Buenos Aires may be objectively measured is by the use of a simple gravity model as discussed in the chapter on transport, p. 69.

EXERCISE 2.   Test the rank size rule for the first five cities of the countries of Europe and compare the results with those for the countries of Africa and Latin America.

EXERCISE 3.   **Sphere of Influence.**—Fundamental to central place theory is an area around the settlement which comes within its economic and social influence. This area, synonymous with the hinterland of a port, is normally referred to as the sphere of influence and will vary with the size and function of the central place and with competing settlements of similar or greater size around it. The relationship between size of settlement and its sphere of influence is shown graphically by Berry and is reproduced in Fig. 5.9 and is apparent too in the Table 5.3. Size alone cannot be regarded as the sole criterion in delimiting a sphere of influence for the recent coalfield or industrial town may not have the urban equipment (see Chap. 6) comparable to its size and may have a much smaller area of influence than the long established market town of similar size.

Methods of delimiting the sphere of influence

It is proposed here only to discuss briefly (*a*) methods based on the town function itself and (*b*) methods based on village data since these are all well known and literature on them is readily available. Methods based on the application of Reilly's Law of Retail Gravitation and that of Huff's Probability Model are treated in a more detailed way so that they may be used in a wider context by readers.

1. The Town Function as a Base

Nearly all such methods attempt to delimit the area served by the town through the use of specific criteria

agent not for the town alone but for the surrounding area too.

An alternative method is to use the links between the town and countryside as expressed in the bus services. Simple isochrone maps may be drawn on the basis of frequency and/or time taken to reach various villages and a distance decay factor observed, *i.e.* a diminishing influence with increasing distance from the centre. This technique may be extended to derive an index of accessibility by dividing the time

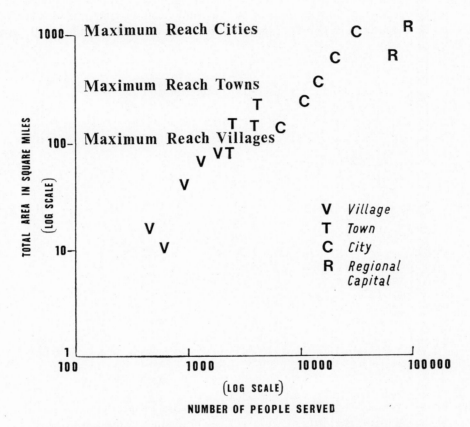

FIG. 5.9. Trading areas and number of people served by differing levels of the hierarchy.
Source. Berry: *Geography of Market Centres and Retail Distribution*, p. 27.

or by determining the accessibility of surrounding villages through the frequency of local bus services. The types of criteria chosen include: area served by shops and schools, area covered by the circulation of the local newspaper or by business functions such as banks and insurance companies. According to the criterion chosen so the size of the area will vary and perhaps the most useful measure to choose for one's local town is that of the newspaper circulation, since the newspaper itself is both a collecting and diffusion

taken to reach a certain village by the frequency of buses travelling to that village. By plotting a series of these indices, isopleths of accessibility and hence influence may be interpolated. A worked example of this technique for villages, south of Lincoln, using the map extract No. 1, is shown in Fig. 5.10. The indices were derived by using the timetable of the Lincolnshire Road Car Company in the way specified above and the result plotted on the $\frac{1}{4}$-in. scale, *e.g.* Leadenham is 45 minutes from Lincoln and the normal daily frequency is 16, giving an index of 2·8. Care must be taken in extracting frequencies from timetables as villages are sometimes located on more than one route, *e.g.* Branston is thirteen minutes away from the city but on four routes.

It may be seen from Fig. 5.10 that there is a definite distance decay factor operating, sometimes as a uniform progression, e.g. along the A607, but frequently in a stepped pattern reflecting the duplication of routes serving some villages. The focal nature of Lincoln is emphasised by the low indices immediately around it (due to being served by several bus routes converging on the city) just as the high indices indicate the relative inaccessibility of those peripheral villages

were listed and according to whether or not they were obtained in the focal town, points were awarded at the rate of one per service, *e.g.* if Milverton (1326) obtained twelve of its services in Taunton it would be allocated twelve points. Where services are provided by two towns, *e.g.* Taunton and Wellington, points awarded were halved. In theory then a village could score a maximum of fifteen. Scores were plotted and isopleths drawn to show zones of dependency. The work of Bracey on two towns is shown in Fig. 5.11. The decrease of a town's influence with distance is evident as is the strength of a competing settlement. This is a relatively simple if laborious exercise which could form part of a local

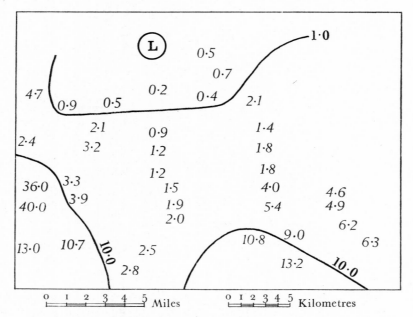

FIG. 5.10.   Accessibility indices of Lincolnshire villages.   (See Map 1.)

not located on the A roads connecting Lincoln with adjacent towns such as Newark, Grantham, and Sleaford. This index provides a stronger measure of accessibility than one based on either time or distance alone and can be simply calculated for any rural locality. It may be interesting to compare the three zones indicated with those of Bracey's work on Somerset which is considered below.

2. The Countryside as a Base

The classic work is that of Bracey who measured the impact of the town upon individual villages. Fifteen services ranging from clothing to dentists considered normal to the requirements of village dwellers

field work programme. A suitable questionnaire for such a survey may be found at the end of this chapter.

Reilly's Law of Retail Gravitation.—The attraction of an individual settlement will depend partially upon its size and hence "urban equipment" (this will be developed in the next chapter), its distance from other similar centres, and the presence of an intervening opportunity. Where one has a county town such as Hereford or Taunton it is possible to generate their sphere of influence by using Reilly's "breaking point" equation which establishes the trade area boundary between two towns. If we have two towns *A* (large) and *B* (small) then the breaking point in miles from the smaller town B is determined by the formula

Distance in miles between Town A and Town B

$$\frac{\text{Distance in miles between Town } A \text{ and Town } B}{1 + \sqrt{\dfrac{\text{Population } A}{\text{Population } B}}}$$

for example, on Map 3 Hereford (43,950) and Leo-

Mare corroborates the findings of Bracey, who used empirical means. This point, 7·9 miles from Bridgwater, coincides with Highbridge, shown in Fig. 5.11 to be less than one-third dependent on either Weston or Bridgwater.

The method may be extended to determine the breaking point between a central place such as

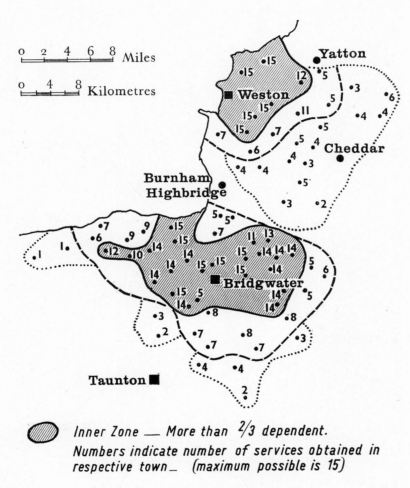

Inner Zone — More than $\frac{2}{3}$ dependent.

Numbers indicate number of services obtained in respective town — (maximum possible is 15)

FIG. 5.11. Trading areas of Bridgwater and Weston delimited by Bracey.
Source: Rutherford, Logan, and Missen, *New Viewpoints in Economic Geography*, p. 385. Based on *I.B.G.*, No. 19, 1953, Fig. 1.

minster (6,830) are thirteen miles apart. The breaking point between the two would be calculated from Leominster as

$$\frac{13}{1 + \sqrt{\frac{43950}{6850}}} = 3\cdot 7 \text{ miles.}$$

It is interesting that the breaking point established in this way between Bridgwater and Weston-super-

Taunton and a series of surrounding towns and so generate a sphere of influence. That arrived at for Taunton in this way is shown in Fig. 5.12 based upon the data in Table 5.4. Although only tentative this sphere of influence is perhaps as valid as that generated by other means and applying other criteria.

EXERCISE. With the help of the population and mileage data contained in Chapter 7, generate a sphere of influence for the county town of Hereford.

In more urbanised areas, however, the tidy arrangement resulting from the breaking point theory is not realistic since time and distance factors do not necessarily predominate over the intervening opportunity provided by the presence of other towns. Two methods may be adopted to show the attraction of various centres and these may be conveniently called the urban case of Reilly's Law and the Huff Probability Model.

TABLE 5.4

Central Place	Population	Adjacent Town	Population	Distance Separating Towns (miles)	Breaking Point Distance (miles)
Taunton	37,120	Bridgwater	26,500	11	5·0
		Chard	6,690	16	4·8
		Honiton	5,110	18	4·8
		Ilminster	2,800	12	2·5
		Watchet	2,600	17	3·5
		Wellington	8,000	7	2·25

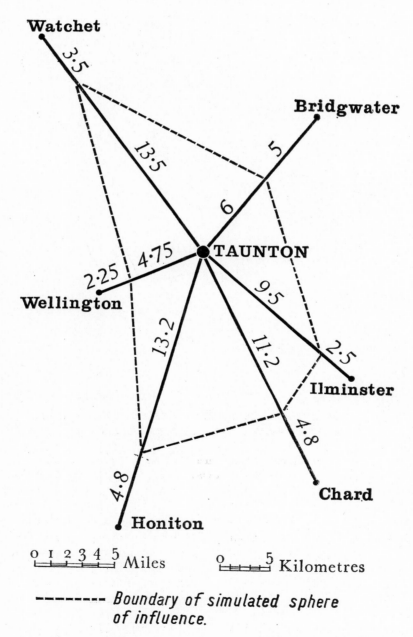

O 1 2 3 4 5 Miles   O ___ 5 Kilometres

------- Boundary of simulated sphere of influence.

FIG. 5.12.   Sphere of influence of Taunton based upon "Breaking Point Theory".

3. The Relative Attractions of Towns

Urban case of Reilly's Law.—Reilly's original law of retail gravitation states, "Two centres attract trade from intermediate places approximately in direct proportion to the size of the centres and in inverse proportion to the square of the distance from these two centres to the intermediate place". This may be expressed in the general formula.

$$\frac{\text{Volume of A's retail trade to B}}{\text{Volume of A's retail trade to C}} = \frac{\text{Pop. B}}{\text{Pop. C}} \times \left(\frac{\text{Distance from A to C}}{\text{Distance from A to B}}\right)^2$$

An example using three Staffordshire towns—Stafford (47,814) is sixteen miles distant from Stoke-on-Trent (276,300) and seventeen miles distant from Wolverhampton (150,385). We wish to determine the proportion of retail trade attracted from Stafford to Stoke and Wolverhampton respectively. This may be accomplished by use of the formula:

$$\frac{\text{Volume of Stafford's retail trade to Stoke}}{\text{Volume of Stafford's retail trade to Wolverhampton}}$$

$$= \frac{276,000}{150,000} \times \left(\frac{17}{16}\right)^2 = 2\cdot1$$

From this we may reasonably deduce that the attraction and hence influence of Stoke-on-Trent is just over twice that of Wolverhampton for people living in Stafford.

Huff's Probability Model

The work of Reilly has been described as too deterministic and certainly in the last example it could rightly be argued that the attraction of Stafford itself was not assessed. Huff's model attempts to predict the probability of people's purchasing habits. In the example which follows instead of using population as an index, one commodity—clothing—has been selected from the Census of Distribution to show how this may be used for a specific purpose. We are attempting to predict the probability of people living in Stafford purchasing clothing in (*a*) Stafford, (*b*) Wolverhampton, and (*c*) Stoke-on-Trent. The number of clothing shops in the towns as shown in the Census of Distribution is Stafford 119, Wolverhampton 133, and Stoke 77. In the latter two towns only the shops listed as in the central shopping area have been taken into account since it is unlikely that visitors would be attracted to peripheral shops. Notice too that no account is taken of the size of the shop or indeed of its fashion and this is a limitation upon the model as worked here. Distance rather than time is being used as a factor in the calculations,

again because of the difficulty of finding travelling times except for public transport. The distance to reach shops in Stafford is regarded as one mile and being an arbitrary distance is a further limitation. The Huff formula for the general case is:

Probability that consumer from Centre 1 will purchase goods in Centre 1 is

$$\frac{\dfrac{\text{Number of shops in Centre 1}}{\text{Total time taken or distance travelled to reach them}}}{\dfrac{\text{Total number of the shops in the study area}}{\text{Total time taken or distance travelled to reach them}}}$$

This formula may be adapted as below and must be applied for all the centres in turn. In more sophisticated examples isopleths of probability for the centres may be drawn, but this is not attempted in our example.

Example. Probability that a consumer at Stafford will visit Stafford to purchase clothing is:

$$\frac{\dfrac{\text{Number of clothing shops in Stafford}}{\text{Distance travelled to reach them}}}{\dfrac{\text{Total number of clothing shops in the three towns}}{\text{Total distance travelled to reach them.}}}$$

by use of the data above we are now able to substitute

$$\frac{\frac{119}{1}}{\frac{329}{33}} = \frac{119}{9\cdot9} = 11\cdot9$$

Similar calculations are then made to determine the probability of consumers living in Stafford purchasing clothing in Stoke and Wolverhampton by substituting the respective numbers of clothing shops on the top line of the formula and of course entering the distance separating Stafford from the particular town. Values of 0·5 and 0·8 were obtained respectively for Stoke and Wolverhampton. The sum of probability values must always equal 1 and it is necessary to convert these raw figures as follows: for Stafford to 0·9, for Stoke to 0·04, and for Wolverhampton, to 0·06. This is achieved by adding the raw figures of 11·9, 0·5, and 0·8, expressing each as a percentage of the total and dividing by 100. In real terms the results imply there is a 90% probability that people living in Stafford will buy their clothes in that town, a 6% probability of purchasing clothes in Wolverhampton, and only a 4% probability of visiting Stoke for this specific purpose.

A variety of ways of endeavouring to define the urban sphere of influence have been described and examples given to expose the strengths and weaknesses of each. Whatever method is adopted and applied can at best only indicate the probable sphere of influence since much will depend upon the prowess of the individual entrepreneur and the resultant degree of competition and attraction.

VILLAGE SURVEY IN SOCIO-ECONOMIC GEOGRAPHY

Name of Village   *Number of House*

1. Where do you go to buy the following:
   - (*a*) groceries   (*c*) bread
   - (*b*) milk   (*d*) meat

2. Where do you shop for:
   - (*a*) hardware   (*e*) furniture
   - (*b*) shoes   (*f*) electrical goods (TV.)
   - (*c*) men's clothes   (*g*) hairdressing
   - (*d*) women's clothes   (*h*) fuel

3. Where do you obtain the following services:
   - (*a*) dentist   (*d*) chemist
   - (*b*) doctor   (*e*) hospital
   - (*c*) optician

4. Where do you obtain the following services:
   - (*a*) lawyer   (*d*) veterinary surgeon
   - (*b*) accountant   (*e*) banking
   - (*c*) auctioneer

5. Where is your nearest:
   - (*a*) post office   (*b*) policeman

6. Where do you go for the following entertainments:
   - (*a*) cinema   (*d*) bingo
   - (*b*) theatre   (*e*) public house
   - (*c*) dancing   (*f*) sports fixture

7. Which place of worship do you attend?

8. Which Secondary School do your children attend?

9. Do you own a car? Can you obtain petrol in the village?

10. Where is your place of work? What type of work do you do?

11. What is your means of travel—car/bus/cycle/walk.

12. From which town is your local newspaper delivered?

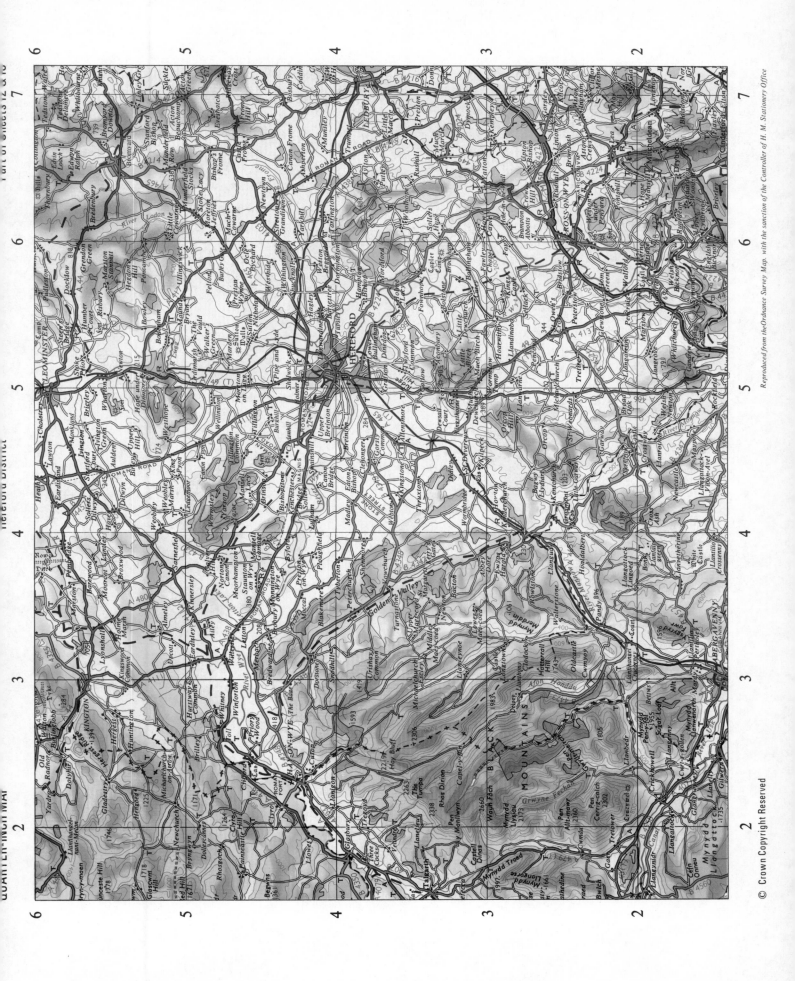

CHAPTER 6

MORPHOLOGY AND FUNCTION OF THE INDIVIDUAL TOWN

Introduction. Some Inherent Problems of Urban Investigation. Models of Urban Structure. The Functions of a Town. 1. Commercial Functions. Correlation Methods. Spearman Rank Correlation Coefficient. 2. Residential Functions. Questionnaire for Socio-Economic Survey in Urban Areas. Usefulness of the Survey. Evaluation of the Sample.

Introduction

Towns are an important feature of the total landscape. In England in 1801 the population classified as urban amounted to 16·9%, whilst for 1961 the total reached 80%. The importance of urban studies in any consideration of the landscape is therefore evident. In this chapter we are concerned with the structure and function of individual towns as revealed by their morphology. It is not intended that the approach should be either historical or descriptive alone, but should incorporate the theoretical structure of towns, the models of which may be tested against reality. Often an investigation of this nature throws the geographer back to the axiomatic principles of sound fieldwork and suggestions are therefore included upon the means of carrying out fieldwork to test theories and concepts. The urban land use map forms only the basis upon which to work and can never be regarded as an end in itself.

Some Inherent Problems of Urban Investigation

The first problem facing the individual or team of investigators is that of mere scale in terms of area or distance, and except in the case of the small market town, transects or sample areas must be used to portray the urban landscape. Associated with this problem is that of complexity—not only in terms of functional use of urban land but also in the social characteristics of the resident population. In the British city, growth patterns are not always easy to detect through direct observation since urban renewal and decay frequently exist side by side. Provision of transport within an urban area and its consequent effect upon degrees of accessibility further complicates the morphology.

The search for order or repetitive pattern is limited too by the distinctive physical features of the individual town, especially the presence of a river or group of hills. Finally, the dynamic force of geography expresses itself dramatically in the urban scene: we are conscious not only of space as a factor but also time as a major concept to be taken into account in any analysis of the landscape. Despite these difficulties attempts have been made to produce models of urban development which are now discussed.

Models of Urban Structure

The Concentric Zone Theory of Burgess.—This is the simplest and most generalised of the three models to be discussed and within the limitations which Burgess himself recognised provides a starting point for investigating a small market town. Outside the central business district, synonymous with the town centre [Fig. 6.1 (*a*)] is located a transition zone containing many older houses, at present often being broken into flats. It is here too that many of the original industries of the town were located and currently are being demolished to allow the C.B.D. to expand. Outside this area are three residential zones which reflect increasing mobility with increasing affluence. This is evident in many smaller British towns. The morphology of Ely [Fig. 6.1 (*b*)] shows some similarity to the Burgess model in that zones are present but appear in reality as isolated patches rather than continuous rings. The open area marked *P* is due to the presence of the Cathedral Close in Ely and can be seen again in association with the Abbey in Bury St Edmunds and the castle in Thetford.

The Sector Theory of Hoyt.—Hoyt's theory may be regarded as a development of that of Burgess. He presupposed growth and development would take place along certain transport axes—roads, railways, or waterways. This may be seen from the star-shaped form of many cities as opposed to idealised circular shapes. The tendency for a particular type of house to predominate in an area may be observed in many towns. Two contrasting residential areas, forming distinctive homogeneous units within one town, are discussed later in this chapter. The agglomeration

THEORETICAL MODEL

EMPIRICAL EXAMPLE

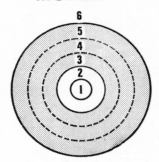

BURGESS: Concentric Ring Theory

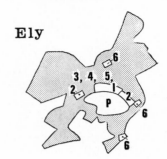

Ely

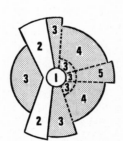

HOYT' Sector Theory

Bury St. Edmunds

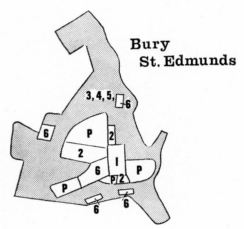

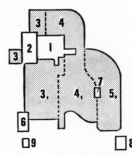

ULLMANN: Multiple Nuclei Theory

Thetford

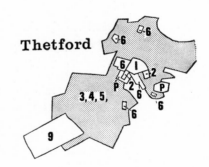

1_ *Central Business District.*
2_ *Commercial / Wholesale,*
    Light Manufacturing/
    "Twilight" Transition.
9 _ *Industrial Suburb*
10 _ *Commuter Zone.*

3_ *Low Class* ⎫
4_ *Middle Class* ⎬ *Residential Areas*
5_ *High Class* ⎭
6_ *Manufacture.*
7_ *Outlying Business District.*
8_ *Suburban Residential Area*
P_ *Public Buildings and Parks.*

FIGS. 6.1, 6.2, and 6.3.   Field testing of hypothetical models.

tendencies evident in industrial patterns repeat themselves in functional patterns of land use in urban areas, *e.g.* industrial quarter and low-class residential area. When analysing British towns it is often advantageous to combine both zones and sectors as in the case of Bury St Edmunds [Fig. 6.2 (*b*)] where evidence of an arrangement of functions in zones within sectors may be detected.

The Multiple Nuclei Model of Ullmann.—An attempt to come to terms with the complexity of urban patterns is embodied in this model which suggests cities have a number of growth points in addition to the C.B.D., *e.g.* a new-type trading estate, the quayside of a port, a suburban shopping

(Fig. 6.4) assumes more than one growth point from the time of its inception.

The Planned Town.—The morphology of the planned "new town" such as Harlow (Fig. 6.4) incorporates elements of all the three basic models. Two broad zones may be recognised as circumscribing the C.B.D. which contains all the administrative offices of the town in addition to the complete range of shops. Adjacent to the C.B.D. is a residential zone where all social groups and hence types of houses are deliberately intermingled to form neighbourhood units, each with its educational and essential shopping facilities. Each of these neighbourhood units is planned to be self-contained. Beyond the residen-

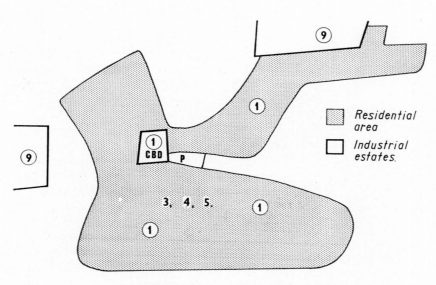

FIG. 6.4.   Function zones in Harlow New Town.

centre, or a distinctive unit such as the jewellery quarter of Birmingham. Similarly, some activities repel others, *e.g.* if a high class residential area develops in a physically desirable site such as higher land on the western side of a British city then it is most unlikely that heavy industry will be allowed to develop adjacent to it. An example is found in Sheffield with its residential suburbs on the west with the heavy industrial development found particularly on the north and east. Fieldwork in Thetford revealed twin nuclei of the C.B.D. with its smaller industries, together with nineteenth century and interwar residential areas, and the modern industrial estate with its consequent post war residential growth. A planned town such as that of Harlow

tial zone are found two industrial estates and since they are located in relation to available transport, they are contained within sectors of this peripheral zone. Each of the industrial estates is a potential nucleus for expansion.

Factors contributing to current land use patterns in urban areas.—The present pattern cannot be fully appreciated without tracing the history of a town's growth. From this will emerge the part played by individual entrepreneurs, particularly in establishing industry. Although some industrial locations may have been related to rivers or railways, many sites could not be accounted for on a purely rational economic basis. Whatever chance or physical element may have led to the establishment of an industry in a particular part of a town, certain consequences followed such a development, viz. the attraction of lower class housing and the repelling of high class housing. This tendency towards separation was earlier modified by Howard in the "garden city" concept and has been recently emphasised by sociologists through the deliberate action of planners in creating neighbourhood units containing a social cross-section of the community. This can be clearly seen in the function map of Harlow (Fig. 6.4).

In addition to physical, social, and chance elements, the economics of land values play a significant role in the ordering of a morphological

now be analysed with reference to the three basic models used either individually or more appropriately in conjunction with each other. From such a study a certain order may emerge from an apparently bewildering map and this pattern may profitably be compared with those of other towns [see Figs. 6.1 (*b*), 6.2 (*b*), 6.3 (*b*)].

The Function of a Town

Although the functions of a town are many perhaps the three most important groups are those classified as commercial, industrial, and residential. Here attention is confined to the commercial and residential functions only since industry has already been considered in Chapter 3.

Commercial Functions

The C.B.D. of a town summarises its commercial functions as expressed in numbers, types, and spatial arrangement of the various shops and offices. The criteria used for delimiting the C.B.D. are discussed by Murphy and Vance in *Economic Geography*, Vol. 30, but the area where retailing of goods, provision of services, and administrative functions predominate over all others may serve as a working basis for establishing the C.B.D. This boundary in common with many other geographical boundaries, would appear as a zone rather than as a line demarcating an abrupt change in land use. Certain characteristics are common to the C.B.D. of any town: departmental stores, supermarkets, specialist shops, services and restaurants, professional establishments such as banks, the administrative offices of local government, and places of entertainment. In older towns will be found the parish church or cathedral, the castle, and a wide open space formerly occupied by the market. Such a spatial arrangement was a common feature of the morphology of the preindustrial town.

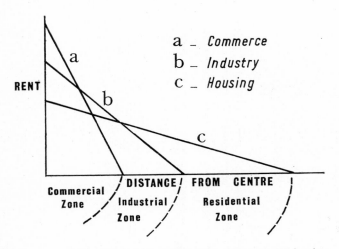

FIG. 6.5. Graph showing the relationships between land values and land use in urban areas.

pattern. The higher the value of a site then the higher the rent that will be charged. Particular activities, however, can only afford to pay a certain rent and assuming the most valuable sites to be in the C.B.D., the graphs in Fig. 6.5 indicate the underlying economic principle of urban land use. This arrangement of graphs is grossly over-simplified since values do not show a straightforward relationship with distance from the town centre but may be interrupted by local areas of a highly desirable nature. At least there is some evidence for the trend in general and this varying intensity of land use with distance from the centre may be tested in reality as illustrated later.

No instructions are included in this section for land use mapping in urban areas as schemes are already abundant in available literature on fieldwork. However resultant morphological/function maps may

The variety and numbers of shops to be found in the individual town is known as its urban equipment. It is related to the population of the town and its catchment area. Hence the importance of determining the tributary area of the town as explained in Chapter 5.

Two factors have a strong influence upon the amount of urban equipment and its spatial arrangement within the town. The first of these is the number of people required to support a particular type of shop, *e.g.* far more people are required to support a jeweller's establishment than a baker's. The minimum number of people required to support a particular function is called the threshold and some ideas of such thresholds are given in the tables below, 6.1 (*a*) and (*b*).

TABLE 6.1 (*a*)

THRESHOLDS OF SEVERAL WELL-KNOWN SHOPS

SHOP	THRESHOLD
Boots the Chemists	10,000
MacFisheries	25,000
Barratts Ltd (Shoes)	20-30,000
Sainsbury's (Grocers)	60,000 (for medium-sized self-service store)
Marks & Spencer's	50-100,000
John Lewis	50,000 (for a supermarket)
John Lewis	100,000 (for a departmental store)

Source: Frontiers in Geography by Chorley and Haggett, p. 227.

TABLE 6.1 (*b*)

THRESHOLD POPULATION FOR SELECTED FUNCTIONS IN S. ONTARIO

FUNCTION	THRESHOLD
General food stores	65
General clothing	85
Banks	727
Lawyers	742
Dentists	1,734
Opticians	2,890

Source: An Introduction to Quantitative Analysis in Economic Geography by Yeates, p. 105.

It should be remembered that the threshold indicates the minimum number of people required to support one establishment and it is unreasonable to assume that a population double this minimum would support two such establishments since the one is capable of catering for far more than the minimum.

The second influencing factor is that known as the range of good or the distance people will travel to obtain a particular good or service. The shopping trips made by residents in Schwamendingen—a suburb of Zurich—were analysed by H. Carol (*I.G.U. Symposium in Urban Geography*, 1962, p. 564). This survey revealed that over 80% of all foodstuffs were purchased in the immediate neighbourhood whilst 60-80% of the population used the C.B.D. to obtain furniture and clothing. In a study of the retail distribution in East Riding of Yorkshire, Tarrant found that 40-50% of the village population obtained their bread and groceries within the village whilst for clothes and furniture 100% used towns or cities and between 75 and 80% used the primate city of the region—Hull. Clearly it is reasonable to expect this trend to be reflected in the retail structure of both the suburban shopping centre and the C.B.D.

Land use mapping in urban areas provides adequate data for testing many of the concepts outlined.

A threshold test may be applied to establish the validity of the figures in Table 6.1 (*a*). This was done for selected towns in eastern England, and whilst a marked relationship was revealed with the population of the town itself, equally the importance of the catchment area is seen in that Bury St Edmunds scored 3 against Harlow's score of 2. The shops scoring one point each by their presence in a town were: Boots, MacFisheries, Marks & Spencer's, Sainsbury's, and John Lewis. See Table 6.2.

TABLE 6.2

SUMMARY OF URBAN EQUIPMENT FOR SELECTED TOWNS IN EASTERN ENGLAND

Town	Population	1	2	3	4	5	T	Total
Cambridge ..	99,830	215	159	150	60	76	5	965
Harlow	68,740	86	52	30	10	38	2	317
Bury St Edmunds	23,690	33	30	19	5	27	3	167
Ely	10,010	22	14	11	3	16	1	108
Thetford	9,730	10	9	3	2	9	0	85

Key: 1, Food shops; 2, clothing shops; 3, household goods; 4, luxury goods; 5, commercial services; T, threshold test (for explanation see text). Total = Total number of all retail establishments.

The range of a good may be appreciated in three ways; (*a*) by comparing the number of shops in the five basic categories for the individual towns as classified in Table 6.2. The shops dealing with luxury goods are fewer in number than clothing shops which in turn are outnumbered by food shops. This pattern is repeated in each of the five towns, indicating that people are prepared to travel greater distances to obtain some goods than for others; (*b*) by comparing the types of shop in a neighbourhood unit or suburban shopping centre with those of the C.B.D. Often one finds as in Harlow, a predominance of food shops with one establishment for each of the essential services such as hairdressing, dry cleaning, hardware, and pharmacy in the neighbourhood unit whilst the C.B.D. contains the full range of urban equipment; (*c*) by establishing through a sample questionnaire the distance people travel for certain goods, *e.g.* twenty out of thirty people questioned in the low class residential district of one town obtained groceries in the immediate neighbourhood but all shopped in the town centre for clothes.

Intensity of commercial land use may also be deduced from a morphological survey. The town may be divided into distance zones using the centre as the point of origin and the number of buildings which have 5, 4, 3, or 2 stories counted for each zone. The concept of decreasing intensity with increasing distance from the centre may be tested. This is known as the distance decay concept. A detailed survey would indicate the varied uses of different floors and ideas of economic rent may be appreciated. Insurance offices are a good example of the use of upper floors, whilst in part of "The High" in Oxford undergraduate rooms are found over shops situated on the ground floor.

Agglomeration or dispersion tendencies may be measured in larger towns by determining the mean distance separating (a) grocers, (b) banks, (c) jewellers, (d) post offices. The agglomeration of doctors in Harley Street and tailors in Savile Row is well known. Garages may be plotted in relation to arterial roads and any evidence for skid-row tendencies evaluated.

Investigation must frequently be confined to one town, but comparisons with other urban areas are made possible by using the Census of Distribution (see Appendix 1). Table 6.2 summarises not only fieldwork results but incorporates information from this Census. Although the towns range in type from a university city, a country market town, and an overspill town to a completely planned new town, a marked relationship between the number of retail amenities and population is revealed and this hierarchical order is perpetuated throughout the five categories of shops. With interval data of this kind, however, it is possible to apply stronger statistical tests and determine the degrees of correlation as is shown below.

Correlation Methods

Correlation techniques enable the statistical relationship between two sets of figures to be established, but it must be stressed that this is not necessarily a causal relationship. When a close relationship is revealed between two sets of figures then the geographer must use his own methodology to establish whether or not this relationship is causal.

Details and a worked example are given of two tests: the Spearman Rank Correlation Test and the Pearson Product Moment Test. In both cases the coefficient of correlation (known as r) will range between $+1$ and -1 and the closeness of approximation to 1 is a measure of the closeness of the relationship between the two components (e.g. the population of towns and the number of shops found in them). A value of $+1$ indicates a perfect positive correlation whilst -1 indicates a total negative correlation. In both cases it is necessary to establish that the result is not a chance one and this is related to the number of items (known as n). In both examples n is 10 and for the r value to have statistical

significance it must be greater than 0·746 at the 99% confidence level and greater than 0·564 at the 95% confidence level. The term confidence level indicates the likelihood of the answer not being a chance one, i.e. 95% confidence level means the answer is likely not to occur by chance 95 times out of 100. Useful values of statistical significance for varying numbers at the two confidence levels are given in Table 6.3 below.

TABLE 6.3
STATISTICAL SIGNIFICANCE AND CONFIDENCE LEVELS

Number of Items	Values of r at Confidence Levels	
	95%	99%
10	0·564	0·746
15	0·440	0·620
20	0·377	0·534
25	0·336	0·475
30	0·306	0·432

Method 1. The Spearman Rank Correlation Coefficient

Aim. To establish the degree of correlation between the urban equipment as expressed in the total number of retail establishments, and the population for selected towns in the East Midlands.

Data. Population and numbers of shops in each town are obtained from the *Census of Distribution*, Part 5. These details are set down in Table 6.4.

TABLE 6.4.   DATA FOR AND COMPUTATION OF SPEARMAN RANK CORRELATION COEFFICIENT.
COLUMN NUMBER

1	2	3	4	5	6	7
Town	Population	Rank Order	No. of Retail Establishments	Rank Order	d	d^2
Coalville	26,159	8	400	7	1	1
Corby	36,322	7	273	10	−3	9
Derby	132,325	3	1,991	3	0	0
Grantham	25,030	9	362	8	1	1
Heanor	23,867	10	315	9	1	1
Leicester	273,298	2	3,842	2	0	0
Lincoln	77,065	4	898	4	0	0
Nottingham	311,645	1	4,064	1	0	0
Peterborough	62,031	6	777	5	1	1
Scunthorpe	67,257	5	676	6	−1	1
						14

PROCEDURE

(1) Rank both the population and the number of retail establishments as in columns 3 and 5 in Table 6.4 above.

(2) Find the difference in ranking between the two phenomena considered, *i.e.* subtract Column 5 from Column 3 and enter this difference in Column 6.

(3) Square the differences and enter the values in column 7.

(4) Add the figures in column 7 to find the value of Σd^2 (where Σ = the sum of).

(5) Determine the coefficient of correlation by using the formula

$$r = 1 - \frac{6 \, \Sigma \, d^2}{(n^3 - n)}$$

where r is the coefficient of correlation, d is the difference in ranking and n is the number of objects ranked (in this case data for 10 towns)

$$r = 1 - \frac{6 \times 14}{1,000 - 10} = 1 - \frac{84}{990} = 0 \cdot 92.$$

This r value of $+ 0 \cdot 92$ shows there is a marked statistical relationship between the population of

Method 2. The Pearson Product Moment Correlation Coefficient

Although this may be regarded as an alternative to Method 1, a stronger measure of correlation is provided, since differences in actual values are used rather than merely the respective rank orders of the two variables.

Aim. To establish the degree of correlation between the number of people living in a town and the number of retail shops trading in the luxury articles of jewellery, leather, and sports goods.

Data. Population and numbers of shops in this category for each of the selected towns in the West Riding of Yorkshire are obtained from the *Census of Distribution*, Part 4. Details are set down in Table 6.5.

Procedure

1. Add all the populations (known as the X values) in Col. 1 and divide by the number of towns to give the mean (known as $\overline{X}$).

TABLE 6.5

DATA AND COMPUTATION OF THE PEARSON PRODUCT MOMENT CORRELATION COEFFICIENT

Town	COLUMN NUMBER						
	1 Population X values	2 Luxury Shops Y values	3 $X - \overline{X}$ x values	4 $Y - \overline{Y}$ y values	5 x^2 in millions	6 y^2	7 xy
Barnsley ..	74,650	39	−138,047	−38	19,056·97	1,444	5,245,786
Bradford ..	295,768	102	+ 83,071	+25	6,900·79	625	2,076,775
Halifax ..	96,037	33	−116,660	−44	13,609·56	1,936	5,133,040
Harrogate ..	56,332	43	−156,365	−34	24,450·01	1,156	5,316,410
Huddersfield	130,302	47	− 82,395	−30	6,788·936	900	2,471,850
Hull	303,268	80	+ 90,571	+ 3	8,203·106	9	271,713
Leeds	510,597	152	+297,900	+75	88,744·41	5,625	22,342,500
Sheffield ..	493,954	175	+281,257	+98	79,105·50	9,604	27,563,186
Wakefield ..	61,591	32	−151,106	−45	22,833·02	2,025	6,799,770
York	104,468	65	−108,229	−12	11,713·52	144	1,298,748
Totals	2,126,967	768	−3	− 2	281,405·83	23,468	78,519,778

$\overline{X} = 212,697$ $\overline{Y} = 77$

Totals in Cols. 3 and 4 do not sum to zero as $\overline{X}$ and $\overline{Y}$ are corrected to Z sig. figs.

towns and the numbers of retail establishments to be found in them. From the table it is statistically significant at a 99% confidence level. Having established this valid relationship geographers may now concentrate their efforts in finding the causes of this established relationship through their own methodology incorporating the background material contained in the main body of this chapter.

2. Add the number of shops dealing in luxury goods in Col. 2 (known as the Y values) and divide by the number of towns to give the mean (known as $\overline{Y}$).

3. Complete Col. 3 by subtracting $\overline{X}$ from X and call these values x.

4. Complete Col. 4 by subtracting $\overline{Y}$ from Y and call these values y.

5. Square the x values in Col. 3 and enter in Col. 5.

6. Square the y values in Col. 4 and enter in Col. 6.

7. Multiply Col. 3 (x) and Col. 4 (y) and enter in Col. 7.

8. Add all the columns 3 to 7.

9. Determine the coefficient of correlation by using the formula:

$$r = \frac{\Sigma xy}{\sqrt{\Sigma x^2 \Sigma y^2}} = \frac{78,519,778}{\sqrt{281,405,830,000 \times 23,468}}$$

$$r = +0{\cdot}966.$$

Again this value indicates a marked statistically significant relationship at a 99 % confidence level. Had this comparison been made by visual examination and expressed in verbal language, the discrepancies may well have been exaggerated and thus inhibited the geographer in his search to discover a causal relationship. With such a high correlation occurring for a second time between population and numbers of retail establishments, data is now provided upon which to form a hypothesis to be tested scientifically. It is essential, however, to point out the limitations of the original data; no indication is given of the size of the individual shop nor of its importance in terms of annual turnover.

EXERCISE 1. Determine the relationship between the total number of shops and population for the towns in Table 6.2.

EXERCISE 2. Using the census of distribution for your own area, determine the coefficient of correlation between (a) population and the number of food shops, and (b) population and the annual turnover of the food shops for the ten largest towns.

EXERCISE 3. Using the Huff Probability Model (p. 47), the data contained in Table 6.5, and appropriate O.S. map, estimate the probability of people living in Barnsley shopping for luxury goods in (a) Sheffield, (b) Leeds, (c) Bradford, (d) Hull.

The Residential Function of Towns

Since some 80 % of the population of England and Wales live in urban areas the residential function of towns is evident. The tendency for types of function to segregate has already been noted and this remains equally valid for differing types of houses. The models all refer to low-class residential and high-class residential areas. This distinctive grouping is in part due to scale economies effected where many construction units may be standardised, to the catering for a particular income group in a particular area, to the ideas of the individual entrepreneur, and to-day to planning controls. Such segregation is made physically possible by the increased mobility of people to-day whereas in Victorian times only the really wealthy could choose to separate themselves from others.

What objective criteria may be used by the geographical fieldworker to demarcate these individual areas? A specimen questionnaire for carrying out a socio-economic survey indicates some of the criteria which may be used: type of house, number of people living there, shopping, travel, and entertainment habits together with the physical amenities possessed by each household. In addition it is sometimes possible to investigate the employment structure of differing areas. Two characteristics not included are age and education because people are often sensitive about such essentially personal questions.

Procedure for Using the Questionnaire

1. From urban land use maps based upon original fieldwork, decide on areas which you feel are either low-class or high-class residential areas.

2. For each in turn select a sample of houses to be visited. This may be done in a number of ways, but all must effectively minimise or preferably eliminate any bias towards particular houses if such a survey is to be statistically valid. One may use the electoral roll for the polling districts of the ward where all the people are numbered and their addresses given. By calling random numbers (see Table on p. 79) one obtains a list of addresses which is without bias. If a detailed urban land use survey has been carried out it is possible to number all the houses on the morphology map and obtain a random sample in a similar way. Frequently time is at a premium in school fieldwork, and it is quicker to carry out a stratified sample visiting every fifth or tenth house in designated streets.

3. Not all the houses visited will necessarily answer the questionnaire and it is essential to standardise procedure for the "non-respondent" cases. Where random numbers have been used it is possible to have a reserve list of addresses. Where a stratified sample is taken, the next door neighbour may be used.

4. The questionnaire is divided into two parts, which may be used either singly or together. This will depend upon the specific purpose of the survey and also the degree of response. It is essential to

remove ambiguity in the actual questions asked and to keep the questionnaire brief, since accurate answers to fewer questions are of greater value than inaccurate answers to a more detailed survey.

Socio-economic Survey in Urban Areas

Town....... Area........ Classification........

PART A AMENITIES

Is the house detached/semi-detached/terraced/flat?

1. How many people live in the house?
2. For normal household goods, do you mainly shop (a) in the neighbourhood, (b) in a peripheral centre, (c) in the town centre, (d) mobile shop?
3. Do you buy groceries from supermarket/chain-store/ private shop?
4. Do you buy clothes in this town or another?
5. How often each month do you go to (a) cinema, (b) theatre, (c) eat out at restaurant, (d) attend sports fixture?
6. Do you have (a) car, (b) caravan, (c) TV., (d) refrigerator, (e) food mixer, (f) automatic washing machine, (g) telephone, (h) central heating?
7. Do you employ domestic help in the house? Would you employ such help if available?
8. How many times in the last year have you visited (a) Birmingham, (b) Bristol, (c) North Wales/ Cornwall/Lake District/Peak District, (d) London, (e) Scotland, (f) a coastal resort?
9. During the last five years, how many times have you been abroad?

PART B EMPLOYMENT

For the Head of Household only.

1. Name and address of present employer.
2. Nature of the industry (S.I.C.).
3. Nature of the occupation.
4. How long in present employment? Has the industry recently been introduced to the area or is it a long established industry?
5. How do you travel to work?
   (i) Public transport yes/no Bus/rail
   (ii) Own vehicle yes/no
   Bicycle/motor cycle/car
   (iii) On foot yes/no
6. How long does a single journey between home and place of work normally take? (minutes)

7. How far in miles is this journey?
8. Is there any point of congestion on this journey?
9. Does your wife go out to work full time/part time/no?
10. Brief statement about the nature of this work.

TABLE 6.6

NUMERICAL ABSTRACT OF RESULTS FROM TWO CASE STUDIES: TOWN 1, A UNIVERSITY CITY AND TOWN 2 A COUNTRY MARKET TOWN.

The size of the sample in Town 1 was 25 and in Town 2, 30.

Type of House—

	TOWN 1		TOWN 2	
Low-Class Residential Area	No.	Percentage of Sample Total	No.	Percentage of Sample Total
Detached	1	4	2	6
Semi-detached	1	4	2	6
Terraced	20	80	26	87
Flats	3	12	0	0
High-Class Residential Area				
Detached	19	76	26	87
Semi-detached	6	24	4	13
Terraced	0	0	0	0
Flats	0	0	0	0

Amenities Possessed—

Low-Class Residential Area

Number of Amenities	Number of Houses with this Number of Amenities		
1	6	1	14
2	8	2	10
3	4	3	5
4	4	4	1
5	2	5	0
6	1	6	0
7	0	7	0
8	0	8	0

Total number of amenities 65   53
Mean per house 2·6   Mean per house 1·76

High-Class Residential Area

1	0	1	0
2	4	2	1
3	2	3	0
4	7	4	4
5	2	5	4
6	7	6	10
7	3	7	9
8	0	8	2

Total number of amenities 115   176
Mean per house 4·6   Mean per house 5·8

Number of Wives Working—

Low-Class Residential Area			
8	32%	17	57%
High-Class Residential Area			
4	16%	3	10%

The Usefulness of the Survey

Whenever a sample is used the results can only provide an estimate of the characteristics for the areas as a whole.   However, it is a better estimate than the mere intuition which geographers have often relied upon in the past.   Full details of how to evaluate the estimate are given in *Statistical Methods and the Geographer* by Gregory and two examples using the data from the survey are given below.

From the numerical abstract alone we are able to suggest the distribution of characteristics upon some definite evidence and to postulate general trends which are common to both towns.   The high-class residential areas have a far higher percentage of detached houses than other types, whilst terraced dwellings predominate in the low-class residential areas.   Again there is a big discrepancy between amenities in the two districts in both towns and this may be tied into standards of living and the need to provide certain shopping facilities (see the earlier section on the commercial function).   There is a marked difference between the percentage of wives who work in the two areas of both towns.   Since the sample is so small it would be invidious to compare directly the characteristics of one town with those of the other, but sufficient evidence is provided to establish hypotheses about social and economic differences between types of towns and areas of the same town which may be more rigorously tested over a longer period of time and using an adequate size of sample.

Whatever the limitations of this investigation it indicates the methods employed by professional planners and schools of urban studies who are often concerned with collecting data for demarcating areas of urban renewal and determining intensity of occupation.   Such relationships between the variable components may be expressed in the form of correlation matrices invaluable to the professional study.

Evaluation of the Sample

It has been suggested above that the sample provides some evidence upon which to base hypotheses and it is important to establish the reliability of such evidence, *i.e.* with what accuracy do the sample figures enable an estimate of the characteristics for the area as a whole to be made?

Case 1.   *The estimate of wives working in the low-class residental area in Town* 2.

This example looks at only one item in a single sample, *i.e.* the number of wives working and com-

pares it with all other items, in this case the number of wives not working.

To determine the accuracy of the 57% sample figure it is essential to discover the sampling error by using the formula:

$$\text{Sampling Error} = \sqrt{\frac{p \times q}{n}}$$

where p = percentage of items considered (wives working),

q = percentage of items not considered (wives not working),

and n = total number in sample,

$$= \sqrt{\frac{57 \times 43}{30}}$$

$$= \sqrt{\frac{2451}{30}} = \sqrt{81 \cdot 7} \simeq 9\%.$$

It is reasonable to suppose that the number of wives working in this area is 57% of the total $\pm$ 9%, *i.e.* the range will be in the range 48% to 66%. If we further suppose the data conforms to the pattern of the normal distribution curve then this value will have a 68% probability of being correct.   The geographical significance of this estimate must now be evaluated through our own methodology, emphasising that newer techniques are only aids to judgement. The number of wives already working may indicate (*a*) potential female labour or (*b*) the wealth of an area which may affect the potential and actual retail markets.

Case 2.   *To what extent does the sample mean of* 4·6 *amenities possessed per house in the high-class residential area of Town* 1 *enable us to estimate the mean for the area as a whole?*

It is helpful to re-arrange the data as shown in the Table 6.7.   Column 1 merely lists the number of amenities in each individual house contained in the sample.   These are known as the x values and the mean (4.43) as $\bar{x}$.   Column 2 contains the value of x squared to enable the sampling error to be easily determined.   The sampling error in this case may be determined by the formula:

$$\text{S.E.} = \sqrt{\left(\Sigma x^2 - \frac{(\Sigma x)^2}{n}\right) \times \frac{1}{n} \times \frac{1}{n-1}}$$

$$= \sqrt{\left(595 - \frac{13,225}{25}\right) \times \frac{1}{25} \times \frac{1}{24}}$$

$$= \sqrt{\frac{66}{600}}$$

$$= 0 \cdot 331.$$

As before it is reasonable to conclude that the mean number of amenities possessed per house in this district as a whole is $4 \cdot 6 \pm 0 \cdot 33$ and assuming the data conforms to the normal distribution curve then this value will have a 68% probability of being correct.

TABLE 6.7

x	x^2	
2	4	
2	4	
2	4	
2	4	
3	9	
3	9	
4	16	
4	16	
4	16	
4	16	
4	16	$\Sigma x = 115$
4	16	
4	16	$\Sigma x^2 = 595$
5	25	
5	25	$(\Sigma x)^2 = 13{,}225$
6	36	
6	36	$\bar{x} = 4 \cdot 6$
6	36	
6	36	$n = 25$
6	36	
6	36	
6	36	
7	49	
7	49	
7	49	

EXERCISE 1. To what extent is the percentage of detached houses in the sample of the high class residential area in Town 1 an indication of the percentage for the area as a whole?

EXERCISE 2. The mean number of amenities per house in the low class residential area in Town 2 is $1 \cdot 76$ as indicated by the sample. Evaluate this estimate for all the houses in this particular area.

SUGGESTIONS FOR FURTHER READING FOR CHAPTERS 5 AND 6

1. Johnson, J. H. *Urban Geography.* An Introductory Analysis, Pergamon, Oxford, 1967.

2. Rutherford, J., Logan, M.I., and Missen, G. J. *New Viewpoints in Economic Geography*, Harrap, Sydney, 1966.

3. Berry, B. J. L. *Geography of Market Centres and Retail Distribution*, Prentice Hall, New Jersey, 1967.

4. Haggett, P. *Locational Analysis in Human Geography*, Arnold, London, 1965.

5. Yeates. *Introduction to Quantitative Analysis in Economic Geography*, McGraw Hill, New York, 1968.

6. Chorley and Haggett (*Ed*). *Models in Geography*, Methuen, London, 1967.
   (*a*) Chapter 9: "Models of Urban Geography and Settlement Location"—Garner, B. J.
   (*b*) Chapter 14: "Models of Evolution of Spatial Patterns in Human Geography"—Harvey, D. W.

7. Dickinson, R. E. *The City Region in West Europe*, Routledge, London, 1967.

8. Jones, E. *Towns and Cities*, O.U.P., London, 1966.

9. Carter, H. *The Towns of Wales*, University of Wales Press, 1966.

10. Moser, C. A., and Scott, W. *British Towns:* a Statistical Study of their Social and Economic Differences, London, 1961.

11. Murphy, R. E., and Vance, J. E. "Delimiting the C.B.D." *Economic Geography*, **30,** 1954.

12. Bracey, H. E. "Towns as Rural Service Centres, An Index of Centrality with Special Reference to Somerset." *Trans. I.B.G.*, 1953, p. 95-105.

CHAPTER 7

TRANSPORT NETWORKS

The Role of Transport in Geography. Factors Contributing to a Transport Network. Analysis of Transport Networks:— (a) Traditional, (b) Density, (c) Integration, (d) Accessibility. The Use of the Network; (a) Flow Lines—Journey to Work Patterns, (b) the Simple Gravity Model.
Improvements in a Network.

The Role of Transport in Geography

The emphasis upon pattern analysis in modern approaches to geography has brought into sharp focus spatial distributions and spatial relationships. Underlying all distributions is distance, which is described by J. W. Watson as "a measurable phenomenon basic to the study of geography". Our concern in reality is the overcoming of distance in keeping with the principle of least effort, and this implies an efficient transport network operating at minimal cost compatible with demand or desire for movement. Transport media and the accessibility they provide hold the key to locational patterns and every technical advance, such as the building of the motorways or the Severn Bridge, necessitates a re-assessment of spatial relationships which are continually changing through time.

The physical and economic requirements, the relative costs, and the advantages and disadvantages of various transport media have been discussed in many texts and therefore our attention here is confined to patterns of transport networks rather than their use as means of transport.

Factors Contributing to a Transport Network

An extensive analysis of the structure of transport networks has been undertaken by Kansky who identified five independent variables contributing to a particular network. The variable factors he listed as relief, shape, size, population, and degree of economic development. The factors are called variables because they are not constant but vary with period of time and the techniques available at that time. For each factor he devised a statistical scale to facilitate comparisons between regions and countries and an extract is given in Table 7.1. It is proposed to discuss briefly each of those factors elaborating where possible with a worked example using the Hereford Map Extract (Map No. 3).

TABLE 7.1

	Technolo-gical Scale	Demogra-phic Scale	Size	Shape	Relief
Ghana	355	15	4·9	2·5	2·8
France	125	38	5·3	1·4	12·0
Sweden	154	55	5·2	2·8	8·3
Algeria	323	26	5·9	1·2	1·5
Turkey	283	8	5·4	2·6	19·4
Chile	239	24	5·4	3·1	66·8
Malaya	256	17	4·7	2·1	19·5

Source: Extracted from Kansky: *Structure of Transport Networks.*

Relief

By calling random numbers three axes are located across the study region and cross-sections along each axis constructed. For each of the cross-sections the straight line distance is regarded as 100% and the surface distance expressed as a percentage of this (always larger than 100). Add the differences between the two percentages and divide by three to obtain a measure of the relief. One major weakness of this is that whilst it may reflect mountain barriers it would not necessarily reflect rivers or river estuaries which constitute a major barrier to transport in Great Britain. Axes are constructed for the study area of Herefordshire and a figure of 6·3 derived from the measurements recorded in Table 7.2.

TABLE 7.2. A RELIEF INDEX FOR HEREFORDSHIRE

	Straight Line Distance	Per Cent.	Surface Distance	Per Cent.	Difference
Axis 1	1·8	100	1·9	106	6
Axis 2	4·9	100	5·2	106	6
Axis 3	5·7	100	6·1	107	7
					19 ÷ 3 = 6·3

The lower the figure, the more favourable is the relief. One would expect a figure of less than one in the Fens and one must seriously question the validity of such an index in an area where the drainage pattern certainly is a controlling influence upon transport routes. The index of 6·3 for Herefordshire is higher than one would expect on the basis of scale and height of the hills but it reflects the broken nature of the terrain which is, of course, significant in terms of routeways.

Shape

The concept of shape has already been discussed in Chapter 5 and it is reasonable to assume that an elongated country would have a very different transport network than a compact one. An index of shape may be calculated from the formula

$$\text{Shape} = \frac{L}{l}$$

where L is the length of the longest axis (Axis 1 in Fig. 7.1) and l the length of the perpendicular to the boundaries midway along the longest axis (Axis 2 in Fig. 7.1). This may be applied to any region and its simplicity commends its use in preference to other methods. Despite certain weaknesses (a circle and a square both give the same optimal index of 1) this formula provides a measure of compactness for comparison, e.g. the values for five English counties are: Herefordshire 1·2, Wiltshire 1·6, Lancashire 3·9, Cornwall 4·9, and Berkshire 5·1. These may be visually assessed and evaluated statistically by reference to any standard atlas. The areas measured here have all been political ones but different criteria may be chosen to define an area, such as population density, and the technique may be used to analyse the shape of the more populated areas of a country or continent such as Swanland, Central Chile, and the Nile Valley, all of which are surrounded by areas of much lower density.

Size

Size is more important in terms of the media of transport used than of the actual network, although it will be eventually reflected in the density of a particular network, e.g. the distances travelled in Great Britain are so short that canals cannot compete with roads and railways and therefore have declined in comparison with those of continental Europe. Similarly, the challenge of road to rail transport is caused by shortness of haul increasing ton-mile rates due to disproportionate handling costs for such short

journeys. This is reflected in the pruning of the railway network as detailed in the Beeching Plan for the re-shaping of British Railways.

Population

Kansky was concerned with contrasting national areas and devised an index taking into account not only density of population but also relative birth and death rates. In an area such as Herefordshire it is sufficient to note the low population of 138,000 occupying 842,000 square miles. Population density when combined with an appropriate standard of

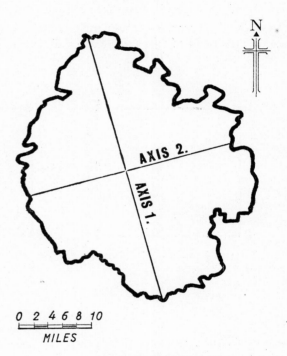

FIG. 7.1. The shape of Herefordshire.

living will be reflected in the use of transport (see later in the chapter) and hence the network, e.g. improvements in the British road network since World War II and especially the building of the motorways reflect these influences.

Technological Scale

Berry has used forty-three measures of economic development and combined them mathematically; the kinds of criteria used for international comparison are energy consumption, income per capita, and exports per capita. The relationship to the stage of economic development is particularly important since this fundamentally determines the purpose of the network. The demands of an agricultural rural society differ from those of the industrialised urban society just as the primitive track differs from the motorway. A strong correlation has been shown to exist between per capita income and the integration of a transport network. What is significant in Herefordshire is the predominantly agricultural nature of the economy and the first impact of industrial overspill from Birmingham in Hereford itself. The spacing of the existing market towns may well be a dominant factor in determining the local road network.

Analysis of Transport Networks

Traditional Approach.—Frequently routeways are related to the relief of an area, *e.g.* the valley routes in

economic development and it is reasonable to assume that in a developed country such as Great Britain a higher density network will exist in city areas than in rural ones. The mileage of the A road network within an area of 25 square miles centred on Hereford is 19½ miles compared with 44 miles for a similar area centred on Birmingham. An American study has proved a high correlation exists between road length and number of junctions, so that a quicker way of determining the road density of a given area is to count the junctions rather than perform the longer task of measuring road length.

EXERCISE. Examine in turn the density of the A road and B road networks within an area of 144 square miles centred upon (*a*) Hereford and (*b*) Pontrilas (6928). To what extent do these results

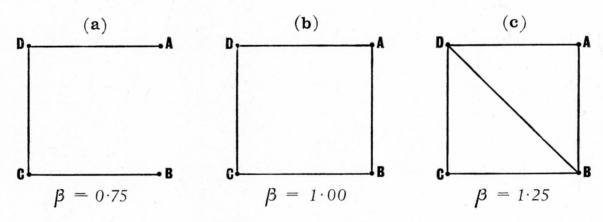

FIG. 7.2.   Increasing degrees of connectivity in a network.

Snowdonia, the pre-historic ridge routes, and the focusing upon gaps and bridging points. This relationship retains its importance, but must be integrated with newer approaches as relief alone cannot explain the overall pattern of communications, nor in some cases of particular routeways. A useful exercise is to examine the relationship between relief and (*a*) A roads and then (*b*) the B roads to the north and west of Hereford.

Density.—Density is usually measured and expressed in terms of length per 100 sq. Km. as in the *Ginsburg Atlas of Economic Development.* That a great disparity exists between countries is revealed in the fact that the range in road density extends from 302 to 0 and that for railways from 17·9 to 0. Density is a measure of population distribution and

confirm the hypothesis that density decreases in a rural area and/or a region of more adverse relief? It is helpful in working this exercise to construct on tracing paper a square 12 miles by 12 miles on the ¼-in. scale, to draw diagonals and place the intersection of these diagonals on the centre of the settlement required.

Integration

The pattern of a particular network may be measured in terms of integration, *i.e.* the number of possible routes which may be used in travelling from *A* to *B*. In Fig. 7.2 (*a*) there is only one very circuitous route joining *A* and *B*, in Fig. 7.2 (*b*) one has a choice of two routes whilst in Fig. 7.2 (*c*) there are three possible routes. There is progressively a higher degree of integration and hence greater accessibility in terms of connectivity, but not necessarily distance, for all places within the network.

Kansky devised several methods of measuring integration; the one selected and applied here is that of the Beta Index. This is particularly useful in that any network with a value of less than one is only partially connected—in Fig. 7.2 (*a*) there is no direct link between *A* and *B* except via *C* and *D*. If the value is 1 then there is only one possible circuit (Fig. 7.2 [*b*]). Higher values above 1 indicate a complex structure and a high degree of integration between places. The Beta Index expresses the relationship between

at that node, *e.g.* in Fig. 7.2 (*c*) *A* = 2, *B* = 3. This aspect will be developed later in the chapter.

Kansky has determined the Beta Indices for the railway networks of 18 randomly selected countries as shown in Fig. 7.3 (*a*) and a strong correlation may be shown between stage of economic development and degree of integration. Four groups of countries emerge each having reached a progressively higher stage of development measured in terms of per capita income. Fig. 7.3 (*b*) gives the Beta value of connectivity for the main international arteries of some European countries. The index of 1·91 for the England and Wales network is derived from the map

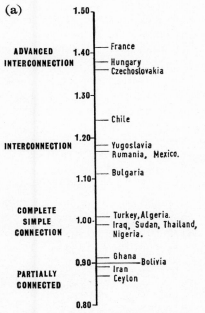

FIG. 7.3 (*a*). Grouping of eighteen selected countries with respect to railroad connectivity.

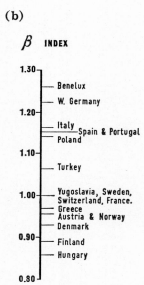

FIG. 7.3 (*b*). Indices of connectivity for the main international arteries of some European countries.

(*Source:* Yeates, *An Introduction to Quantitative Analysis in Economic Geography.*)

edges (*i.e.* the main roads or railways joining two vertices) and vertices. A vertex may be identified as (*a*) a town of origin or destination, (*b*) a major town en route or (*c*) any intersection of two or more roads. The index is expressed in the formula:

$$B = \frac{\text{Edges}}{\text{Vertices (or nodes)}}$$

Examine Fig. 7.2 to see how the Beta Indices indicated there have been derived from the networks shown.

It is possible and often relevant to state the connectivity of an individual vertex in terms of the Beta Index and this is simply the number of edges meeting

showing the projected motorway pattern of the early 1970s, supplemented by comprehensively modernised trunk roads, Fig. 7.4. The degree of integration of this improved road system may thus be statistically compared with that of the other European countries, but it must be remembered that merely connectivity and not actual distances travelled, is taken into account.

Procedure to derive the Beta Index for a Study Area using the O.S. Map.

(1) Reduce the road network to a series of edges and vertices as in Fig. 7.5 which shows in this diagrammatic way the A road network between

Hereford and the remaining market towns of the county.

(2) Care must be taken to retain the correct number of vertices and the correct number of links between them.

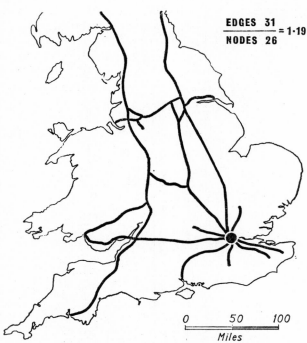

$$\frac{\text{EDGES } 31}{\text{NODES } 26} = 1·19$$

Fig. 7.4. Projected motorway pattern of the early 1970s together with comprehensively modernised trunk roads.
(*Source: The Guardian*).

(3) Count the number of edges and vertices and discover the Beta Index by applying the formula:

Beta Index of A Road Network of Herefordshire

$$= \frac{29 \text{ (edges)}}{21 \text{ (vertices)}} = 1·38.$$

From the worked example we may conclude that this network shows a surprising degree of integration in view of the population density and the agricultural nature of the economy. It may well reflect therefore a national tendency rather than specifically a county one, for one is aware that the study area is circumscribed by a medieval political boundary and a more relevant unit of study would perhaps be the economic planning region.

EXERCISE. To test the hypothesis that the degree of integration in the Taunton area should be of the same order as that for Hereford in view of the similar physical and economic characteristics.

Using map extract 2 on wrap round, determine the degree of integration of the A road network connecting Taunton with the immediately adjacent Somerset towns. To what extent is the Beta Index value comparable to that for Herefordshire?

Accessibility

No account has yet been taken of distance between locations in any of these analyses. One method is fully explained by J. P. Cole in his book on Latin America where the worked example of Peru is given. The Herefordshire example which follows is directly based upon the methods Dr Cole outlines. By comparing road distances between places with direct distances between the same places, it is possible to establish an index of directness for any link in the network. We then have the data to show how some routes are more direct than others and to see where possible improvements may be planned. Furthermore the advantage of a particular location relative to others in the study area, may be evaluated and thus a hierarchy of accessibility revealed. Of course it is fairly easy to perceive, though not evaluate, those advantages visually for a central location such as Hereford, but in a peripheral location one is immediately in difficulties. One cannot judge by eye the relative advantages of Bromyard in comparison with Ledbury—measurement becomes essential.

A mileage matrix of road distances is compiled by measurements from the O.S. Map (Table 7.3) and a

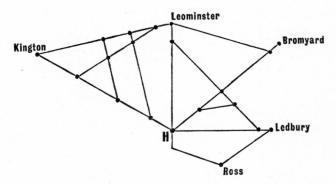

Fig. 7.5. Topological map of the A road network of Herefordshire. (See Map 4.)

similar matrix compiled for direct distance (Table 7.4). An index of directness may then be ascertained by the formula:

$$\text{Index of directness} = \frac{\text{Road distance}}{\text{Direct distance}} \times 100$$

This is again represented in matrix form in Table 7.5.

TABLE 7.3. ROAD DISTANCES BETWEEN MARKET TOWNS IN HEREFORDSHIRE

	Br.	H.	K.	Ld.	Lm.	R.	Totals
Bromyard ..	0	14	26	12	12	24	88
Hereford ..	14	0	20	15	13	15	77
Kington ..	26	20	0	35	14	35	130
Ledbury ..	12	15	35	0	22	12	96
Leominster..	12	13	14	22	0	28	89
Ross	24	15	35	12	28	0	114
Totals	88	77	130	96	89	114	

The totals column indicates the mileage travelled if a series of journeys is made from any one market town to all others in the county, and so can provide some index of the potential of each town as a distribution centre in the county. The hierarchy of accessibility so established is Hereford, Bromyard, Leominster, Ledbury, Ross, and Kington. At this point it is interesting to quote the Beta Index for each of these towns as discussed earlier, viz: Hereford 9, Leominster 5, Ledbury 5, Ross 5, Kington 4, and Bromyard 3. The predominance of Hereford and the important position of Leominster on both scales is a significant feature.

TABLE 7.4

DIRECT DISTANCES BETWEEN MARKET TOWNS IN HEREFORDSHIRE

	Br.	H.	K.	Ld.	Lm.	R.	Totals
Bromyard ..	0	13	22	11	10	19	75
Hereford ..	13	0	17	12	12	12	66
Kington ..	22	17	0	28	13	28	108
Ledbury ..	11	12	28	0	19	11	81
Leominster..	10	12	13	19	0	22	76
Ross	19	12	28	11	22	0	92
Totals.. ..	75	66	108	81	76	92	

The deviations between the totals of direct distance and road distance are: Hereford 11, Bromyard 13, Leominster 13, Ledbury 15, Ross 22, and Kington 22. In the explanation of these deviations there is scope for attempting to relate the pattern to physical features in a purposeful way and of assessing the need for detours to connect smaller settlements not on the direct route when no physical obstacle prevented the building of a direct route between the towns.

The relationship of actual to direct distance may now be used to calculate the index of directness between market towns.
e.g. Hereford—Bromyard Table 7.3 = 14, Table 7.4 = 13.

$$\tfrac{14}{13} \times 100 = 107.$$

TABLE 7.5

INDEX OF DIRECTNESS BETWEEN MARKET TOWNS IN HEREFORDSHIRE

	Br.	H.	K.	Ld.	Lm.	R.	Totals
Bromyard ..	0	107	118	109	120	127	581
Hereford ..	107	0	118	125	108	125	583
Kington ..	118	118	0	125	108	125	594
Ledbury ..	109	125	125	0	115	109	529
Leominster ..	120	108	108	115	0	127	578
Ross	127	125	125	109	127	0	613
Totals	581	583	594	592	583	613	

It is important to note that the lower the number the more direct and hence efficient the link. Perfection would be 100 for individual routes and 500 for the totals. These results are presented in summary form for the county in Table 7.6, *e.g.* Bromyard

$$\tfrac{88}{75} \times 100 = 117.$$

TABLE 7.6

COUNTY SUMMARY OF DISTANCES AND DIRECTNESS

	Total Road	Total Direct	Index of Directness
Bromyard	88	75	117
Hereford	77	66	117
Kington	130	108	120
Ledbury	96	81	119
Leominster	89	76	117
Ross	114	92	124

Deductions which may be made from the Tables

The value of these tables lies in their ability to give some statistical rather than subjective answer to questions often posed by geographers. Also they reveal relationships which a geographer would then seek to explain through his own methodology. Some of the more obvious deductions are as follows.

Hereford not only has the most efficient links with other towns in the county, but is itself the dominant central place in terms of accessibility. All trained geographers would have suspected this after a cursory glance at the map, but would they have been able to prove it, or appreciate its relative efficiency in comparison with other market towns? In fact three other towns are only slightly less well placed to serve the area as a whole. Some indication can therefore be given for the optimum location for both service and distributive industries for the county. This location is Hereford; the other market towns are ranked on a statistical rather than subjective basis indicating the best secondary location for such centres.

Ross and Kington show very poor integration in the Herefordshire network, yet on a map they do not appear markedly more peripheral than Ledbury. This leads to two implications (*a*) the general feature that transport connectivity is orientated to the north and east, which could be the economic axis of the county and (*b*) for Kington it could give some reason for the index of its economic stagnation and static population. It is really necessary to check the integration of Kington in the Radnorshire matrix and if it continued to show poor connectivity, a more powerful measure of its isolation would be available.

The apparent advantage of Ledbury illustrates the importance of deciding upon actual boundaries for a region or study area. An analysis including Hay, Abergavenny, and Monmouth in the area removed this advantage, whilst that of Hereford and Leominster remained. As such, these analyses may show useful economic regions for industries where transport is a major item of cost structure.

The efficiency of any stretch of road is measured in terms of its directness—though not in terms of gradient or surface—and may be compared with any other. This index has immediate application in the planning of future road improvements. Table 7.4 indicates the remarkable uniformity of distance separating the market towns and gives support to long held theories about the development of settlement lattices in rural areas (see Chap. 5).

No account has yet been taken of population and its influence. The role of population in conjunction with distance will be discussed in the gravity model later. Had a weighting been given for population in the accessibility exercises, Hereford (43,950) as opposed to any other town (the next greatest is Leominster 6,830) would far outweigh any other location and population merely supports the evidence of the transport network in establishing the centrality of the county town.

Further ways in which Mileage Matrices help Evaluate Accessibility

The comparison of actual with direct distance and the resultant index of directness is useful in determining the effectiveness of mountains or rivers as barriers to transport. Relevant exercises may be devised for areas such as the Lake District and Snowdonia, or the traditional barrier effect of the Pennines may be measured statistically. The dynamic nature of transport networks was referred to at the beginning of the chapter and the matrix technique may be used to analyse changes in space relations resulting from technological advances as the opening of the Severn and Forth bridges. Full details of such an example—

that of the Severn Bridge—are set out below and the technique could well be applied to predict the change which would take place if the Humber Estuary were to be likewise bridged.

Severn Bridge Accessibility Exercise

Aim.—To determine the change in space relationships resulting from the increase in accessibility at the present time, between pairs of towns on opposite sides of the Severn Estuary, due to the opening of the new bridge.

Procedure and Questions for Discussion

(1) Define the area in which it is proposed to measure the change. In this example a radius of fifty miles from the bridge was used on the basis of local accessibility and especially the welding together of Severnside as a viable economic unit, and the approximate speed of road transport. Assuming that a lorry must return to its place of origin the same day is fifty miles the optimum radius to choose? Would 100 miles prove more rewarding? What criteria would you use to decide this?

(2) Select the towns within the area between which you intend to measure the change. Assuming that all towns generate movement in proportion to their population (see later under gravity model), towns with a population greater than 50,000 were selected. To these were added towns with a special function, *e.g.* the county town of Hereford and the sea-side resort of Weston-Super-Mare. Why?

TABLE 7.7

POPULATION DATA OF SELECTED TOWNS ARRANGED ON A
HIERARCHICAL BASIS

1. Bristol	..	.. 436,000	8. Gloucester..	.. 69,780
2. Cardiff	..	.. 256,900	9. Merthyr-Tydfil	.. 58,800
3. Rhondda ..		.. 141,346	10. Hereford ..	.. 43,950
4. Newport ..		.. 107,780	11. Weston-Super-Mare	42,450
5. Swindon ..		.. 91,430	12. Taunton ..	.. 36,130
6. Bath	..	.. 81,550	13. Monmouth ..	.. 5,720
7. Cheltenham	..	72,930		

In what respects is this population data insufficient to form a picture of the economy of the area? To what extent does the data conform to or deviate from the rank size rule? (Chap. 5).

(3) Construct four matrices (*a*) to show mileages before the opening of the bridge (Table 7.8), (*b*) to show mileages after the opening of the bridge (Table 7.9), (*c*) to show the miles saved on journeys (Table 7.10), (*d*) to show the percentage saving on each journey (Table 7.11). Is mileage the best

TABLE 7.8
MILEAGE MATRIX I—BEFORE OPENING OF BRIDGE

	Bath	Bristol	Cardiff	Cheltenham	Gloucester	Hereford	Merthyr T.	Monmouth	Newport	Rhondda	Swindon	Taunton	Weston-S-M
Bath	0	13	104	43	38	80	107	73	92	111	32	48	32
Bristol	13	0	96	44	35	63	94	60	79	98	41	43	21
Cardiff	104	96	0	65	56	54	24	36	12	12	89	139	117
Cheltenham	43	44	65	0	9	37	68	34	53	72	32	87	65
Gloucester	38	35	56	9	0	28	59	25	44	63	33	78	56
Hereford	80	63	54	37	28	0	43	18	42	58	61	106	84
Merthyr T.	107	94	24	68	59	43	0	34	28	12	92	137	115
Monmouth	73	60	36	34	25	18	34	0	24	40	58	103	81
Newport	92	79	12	53	44	42	28	24	0	19	77	122	100
Rhondda	111	98	12	72	63	58	12	40	19	0	96	141	121
Swindon	32	41	89	32	33	61	92	58	77	96	0	80	62
Taunton	48	43	139	87	78	106	137	103	122	141	80	0	29
Weston-S-M.	32	21	117	65	56	84	115	81	100	121	62	29	0

TABLE 7.9
MILEAGE MATRIX II—AFTER THE OPENING OF BRIDGE

	BA	BR	CA	CH	G	H	MT	MO	N	R	S	T	W-S-M
Bath	0	13	52	43	38	60	73	42	40	68	32	48	32
Bristol	13	0	39	44	35	47	60	29	27	55	41	43	21
Cardiff	52	39	0	65	56	54	24	36	12	12	79	82	60
Cheltenham	43	44	65	0	9	37	68	34	53	72	32	87	65
Gloucester	38	35	56	9	0	28	59	25	44	63	33	78	56
Hereford	60	47	54	37	28	0	43	18	42	58	61	90	68
Merthyr T.	73	60	24	68	59	43	0	34	28	12	92	103	81
Monmouth	42	29	36	34	25	18	34	0	24	40	58	72	50
Newport	40	27	12	53	44	42	28	24	0	19	67	70	48
Rhondda	68	55	12	72	63	58	12	40	19	0	86	98	76
Swindon	32	41	79	32	33	61	92	58	67	86	0	80	62
Taunton	48	43	82	87	78	90	103	72	70	98	80	0	29
Weston-S-M	32	21	60	65	56	68	81	50	48	76	62	29	0

TABLE 7.10
MATRIX III. INCREASED ACCESSIBILITY INDICATED BY SAVING IN MILES PER JOURNEY

	BA	BR	CA	CH	G	H	MT	MO	N	R	S	T	W-S-M
Bath			52			20	34	31	52	43			
Bristol			57			16	34	31	52	43			
Cardiff	52	57									10	57	57
Cheltenham													
Gloucester													
Hereford	20	16										16	16
Merthyr T.	34	34										34	34
Monmouth	31	31										31	31
Newport	52	52									10	52	52
Rhondda	43	43									10	43	45
Swindon			10						10	10			
Taunton			57			16	34	31	52	43			
Weston-S-M			57			16	34	31	52	45			

TABLE 7.11
MATRIX IV. ADVANTAGE EXPRESSED AS A PERCENTAGE SAVING

	BA	BR	CA	CH	G	H	MT	MO	N	R	S	T	W-S-M
Bath			50			25	32	42	57	39			
Bristol			59			25	36	52	66	44			
Cardiff	50	59									11	41	49
Cheltenham													
Gloucester													
Hereford	25	25										15	19
Merthyr T.	32	36										25	29
Monmouth	42	52										30	38
Newport	57	66									13	43	52
Rhondda	39	44									11	31	37
Swindon			11						13	11			
Taunton			41			15	25	30	43	31			
Weston-S-M			49			19	29	38	52	37			

measure to use? Would time/cost be better measures, and if so, how could this data be obtained and how reliable would it be?

(4) Plot on a base map percentage increases in accessibility (Fig. 7.6). Three categories were used here but these are not the only ones which could have been used and in working other examples one

This may be tested in practice by census returns and in theory by application of a gravity model to be introduced later.

The Use of a Network

Flow lines.—Flow line maps based upon traffic census figures indicate the actual use of particular

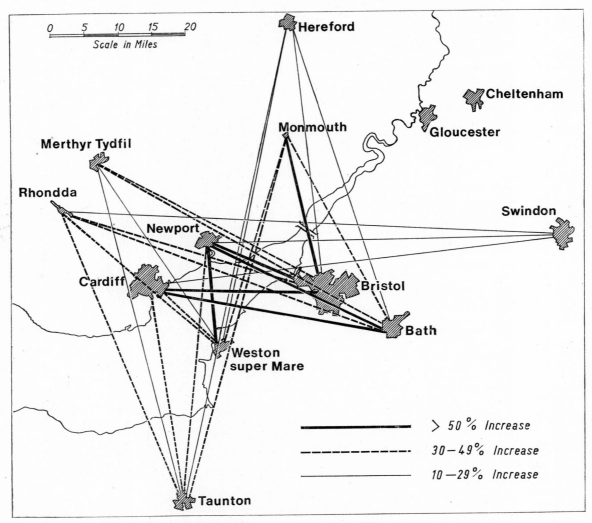

Fig. 7.6. Increased accessibility results from the building of the Severn Bridge.

should try and group categories where there is a marked break in frequency.

(5) What are the likely economic consequences of increases in accessibility? What aspects must you consider and what evidence must you weigh?

(6) To what extent is the greatest saving on those routes where the greatest movement is to be expected?

roads within a network, and details of these maps may be found in books concerned with cartographic techniques as well as in standard regional texts. A more recent approach has been that of graphing journey to work patterns at points along individual roads. These graphs show the number of vehicles (which may be sub-divided into categories relevant to the investigation) which pass the check points during every hour of the day. By comparing a series of them for a particular town it is possible to see where traffic congestion is likely to occur and the extent to which this may be relieved by staggering the hours of travel.

The Simple Gravity Model

In addition to enabling a more penetrating analysis of present patterns to be made, statistical techniques and models may also predict future patterns which may reasonably be expected to emerge. This is particularly important in developing countries where networks are frequently minimal to requirements.

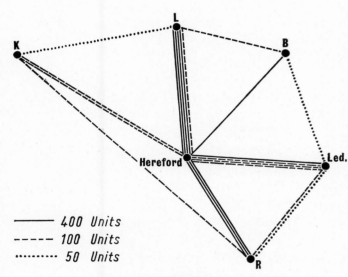

——— *400 Units*
----- *100 Units*
·········· *50 Units*

FIG. 7.7. Predicted flow of movement between the market towns of Herefordshire.

Predictive models may well indicate the optimum use to be made of the limited resources available.

The gravity model is concerned with the amount of movement generated between two locations and this will bear a relationship to the size of the places as expressed in population and the distance separating them. In its simplest form it may be expressed in the formula:

$$\frac{\text{Movement between}}{\text{Towns } A \text{ and } B} = \frac{\text{Population of Town } A \times \text{Population } B}{\text{Square of the distance separating Towns } A \text{ and } B}$$

The results of applying this formula to Herefordshire are shown in Table 7.12 and plotted as desire lines in Fig. 7.7. Again the predominance of Hereford is apparent and the axis of Hereford-Leominster revealed as a potential growth pole for economic

development. It is interesting that this coincides with the A49 trunk road on Map 3. The remoteness of Kington is confirmed.

TABLE 7.12

MATRIX OF DESIRE FOR MOVEMENT IN 000's OF UNITS AS DERIVED FROM THE SIMPLE GRAVITY FORMULA

	Br.	H.	K.	Ld.	Lm.	R.
Bromyard ..	0	376	5	42	80	26
Hereford ..	376	0	209	713	1,776	1,166
Kington ..	5	209	0	6	66	79
Ledbury ..	42	713	6	0	52	151
Leominster ..	80	1,776	66	52	0	57
Ross	26	1,166	79	151	57	0

Such a simple gravity model has many weaknesses when dealing with the real world, but it is an exercise with a scientific method which may be employed in school. More sophisticated models regard population alone as a crude index and many use indices of economic activity. Likewise distance is a weak measure, whereas time taken would at least reflect differences in topography. Again, complicated models include exponents for topography and intervening opportunity.

EXERCISE. Using the population and mileage data provided for the Severn Bridge exercise calculate a desire matrix for journeys between all the towns. To what extent do routes showing the greatest percentage gain in accessibility coincide with those where desire for movement is greatest?

Improvements in a Network

The routes upon which improvements to an existing network may be required are revealed by flow line maps which record the density of use. This may be of value in the construction of dual carriageways. Similarly journey to work graphs provide useful data. The index of directness indicates links which are least efficient and hence where improvements would be beneficial. The gravity model predicts the expected movement between places and is invaluable in the planning of new routeways.

The problem of minimising distance in any new pattern is an acute one but it is possible to compute mathematically the minimum distance network for a specific purpose and an admirable summary of these aspects is given in *Locational Analysis in Human Geography* by P. Haggett, pp. 61-70. He indicates the scale of the problem by stating that there are 479,002,000 possible solutions to finding the shortest cyclic route to connect thirteen cities. The optimum solution is of immense practical value when one remembers the volume of raw materials to be assembled and of finished products and services to be distributed throughout the world.

Exercises on route minimisation are complex except in the case involving only three points. A mechanical method (but by no means an infallible one) is described by Dr Morgan in *Models in Geography*. Applied to the Hereford towns it yields the network shown in Fig. 7.8. For an ideal result all angles at intersections should in fact equal 120. Notice this pattern is the ideal one for the road builder but not necessarily for the road user, since the degree of integration is low.

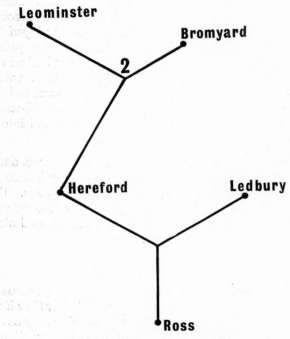

FIG. 7.8. Minimal road networks.

EXERCISE 1. Construct on tracing paper an intersection such as that at 2 in Fig. 7.8. Slide this around on any map to show the minimum distance connecting any three towns, *e.g.* Taunton, Wellington, and Bridgwater on Map 2.

EXERCISE 2. Trace from a map extract the location of several settlements. Attempt to build a road to connect them, travelling the minimum distance. Proceed by (1) joining all the towns without crossing any lines and measure the total distance. (2) Knock out a link and substitute another and see if the total distance is decreased. (3) Proceed to improve the network by trial and error until you reach the most satisfactory one.

Conclusion

It is dangerous practice to isolate any one element in the interpretation of landscape and no false claims are being made in this summary. The geographer is concerned with the whole and must always keep any one factor in perspective and seek to show relationships between factors, *e.g.* the conclusions deduced from a study of transport must be related to ideas of central place theory, spheres of influence, concepts of growth axes, and the characteristics of the present economy if they are to have significant meaning. No suggestion is being made that the real landscape should be sacrificed to mathematical theory. New approaches are built upon past foundations and the intrinsic scientific method of enquiry contained within these quantitative techniques commends them to us in our approach to what remain the fundamental problems of geography.

SUGGESTIONS FOR FURTHER READING

On transport media:

1. Appleton. *Geography of Communications*, O.U.P., London, 1962.

2. O'Dell. *Railways and Geography*, Hutchinson, London, 1956.

3. Manners. "The Pipeline Revolution." *Geography*, **47**, 1962, 154.

4. Sealey. *The Geography of Air Transport*, Hutchinson, London, 1957.

5. Chisholm. *Geography and Economics*, Bell, London, 1966.

On transport networks:

1. Haggett. *Locational Analysis in Human Geography*, Arnold, London, 1965.

2. Chorley and Haggett. *Models in Geography*, Methuen, London, 1967.

3. Kansky. *Structure of Transport Networks*, University of Chicago, 1963.

4. Cole, J. P. *Latin America*, Butterworth, London, 1965.

5. Yeates. *Introduction to Quantitative Analysis in Economic Geography*, McGraw Hill, New York, 1968.

6. Cole and King. *Quantitative Geography*, Wiley, London, 1968.

APPENDIX I

SOURCES: MAPS AND STATISTICS

There is a great mass of information available to-day, so much so, that it is often called a data explosion. Many of the numerous statistics necessary for present day government are now available for general use.

In this Appendix maps are discussed in Section A and statistical sources in Section B.

Section A: Maps

In the table below appears a summary of the British maps that are available. Since prices are often changing these are not listed.

TABLE 1.
BRITISH MAPS

Geological Maps. 1″ Solid and Drift.	Sampling exercises. New Edition covers most of the British Isles.
Topographic Maps. Maps of the whole of Great Britain.	Landform and river studies. Settlement and some limited Land Use studies, *e.g.* distribution of woodlands related to height.
1″ Tourist Sheets of	Ben Nevis, Glen Coe, Cairngorm, Cambridge, Dartmoor, Exmoor, Lake District, Loch Lomond and the Trossachs, New Forest, North York Moors, Peak District, show physical features extremely well.
½″ Map of Norwich.	Transport. Extremely useful for transport and settlement studies.
¼″ Maps of the whole of Great Britain. 2½″ Topographic Maps.	Transport and settlement studies. Excellent for more detailed landform studies.
Land Use Maps. 1″ Map Old Series.	A few sheets of this old series are still available, mainly mountain areas. Land use is shown in six categories. Remaining stocks are held by Edward Stanford Ltd. Maps obtainable in good reference libraries.
2½″ Map New Series.	Excellent detailed maps, land use mapped in 56 categories in eleven colours. About half the series is completed. They are obtainable from Miss. A. Coleman, King's College, Strand, London, W.C.2. and Edward Stanford Ltd, Longacre, London. Methods of using these indicated in Chapter 2.
1 : 100,000 *Maps.*	Administrative Division. These show all the administrative divisions of the counties. Style A shows all the divisions, Style B excludes the Parliamentary Constituencies.
Soil Maps. 1″ Maps.	A series of maps is beginning to be made to cover the whole of the British Isles. The main ones are in North Wales, the Shropshire border lands and the Severn Estuary region. These are useful for relating to agriculture and for sampling.
2½″ Maps.	Isle of Thanet, Church Stretton. The Soil Survey of England and Wales Rothamsted Experimental Station, Harpenden, Herts., produces these maps which are published by the Ordnance Survey.

Town plans with town indices are obtainable for most of the towns of the British Isles from Edward Stanford Ltd., Longacre, London.

Section B: Statistical Data

Although some of the work in this book is based on field work, much basic statistical information exists which can be used in similar ways as in Chapters 4, 5, and 6. This exists in the form of Government, U.N.O., and commercial and industrial reports and year books. In such a survey as this only the main sources can be included with a note on their contents. The sources are listed in subject classes with the U.K. sources first and world sources next.

General Works

Central Statistical Office. Annual Abstract of Statistics, H.M.S.O. 1967, Price £1. 7s. 6d. published annually. The contents range over a great variety of information and give general details for the constituent counties of Great Britain. Population statistics go from 1821-1966 with the geographical distribution of population for urban and rural regions, standard regions, conurbations, and the major cities given from 1911-1966. Fuel and power figures give the coal production, the number of wage earners on the colliery books and output per man-shift for each of the coal mining regions. For the whole of Great Britain there are figures showing the various consumers of coal. Electricity production is included for the years 1956 to 1966 showing the total production by county, the method of generation, and fuel used. Gas production figures showing the fuel used are given for Great Britain for 1956-1966, petroleum supplies and distribution, and output of refineries are listed for 1956-1966.

Details of the production of the main industrial materials, cotton, wool, jute, hemp, timber, leather, woodpulp, fertiliser, dyestuffs, chemicals, man-made fibres, minerals, are given for Great Britain since 1956. The information for the iron and steel industry is much more detailed and contains figures for each producing region since 1956.

Manufacture, construction, agriculture, fishery production statistics, are given for the last ten years.

Information about goods and passenger transport, the roads, the number of vehicles licensed, railway, air, and shipping movements are contained in the transport section. Movement of ships in and out of Britain are given by country of origin.

External trade figures are analysed by source and commodity and principal articles of trade. The labour statistics give information about the number employed in various types of industry.

The Monthly Digest of Statistics gives similar information on a monthly basis.

Historical statistical data on population, labour force, agriculture, coal, including details of the coalfields, iron, steel, tin, copper, building, overseas trade, generally going back to 1800 or even earlier, are given in *Abstract of British Historical Statistics*. Mitchell, B. R., Deare, P., Cambridge, 1962, £2.62½ Central Statistical Office, *Abstract of Regional Statistics*, H.M.S.O. 50p. This has been published since 1965 and gives a breakdown of the statistics by standard regions including employment figures by type of industry, numbers employed, fuel and power production and consumption, steel production, construction of houses, roads, mileages, number of journeys undertaken, foreign trade of the principal ports and coastal trade.

The Statistical Abstract of Ireland, Stationery Office, *Welsh Statistics* and *Scottish Statistics* give similar information.

United Nations Statistical Year Book, New York, published annually, has details of population, agriculture by commodities, forestry, fishing, industrial production mining, and quarrying by mineral, manufacturing by commodity, energy production, trade, transport, and consumption. The figures normally go back to 1948. More detailed population and vital statistics are given in the U.N.O.

Demographic Yearbook. This includes country figures 1947-1966 and the population of capital cities and cities over 100,000.

Similar generalised world statistics are given in Philip, G., *Geographical Digest*, which is published annually. It gives details of recent political changes, changes in places and statistics of population, including the population of major towns, production, trade, and communication. It is a most useful and well arranged book.

Agriculture

Detailed county statistics of agriculture are given in *Annual Agricultural Statistics* produced by the Ministry of Agriculture, Fisheries and Food. Detailed figures of all aspects of agriculture are given for England and Wales. Most useful is the breakdown by counties giving yield per acre, use of agricultural holdings, crops, grass acreage of each holding, size of holding, acreages of each crop and detailed numbers of animals. These figures date back to 1952. Before this the figures were published for the whole country and not for the counties. However, the detailed parish figures may be obtained on the payment of 5p per six items from the Ministry of Agriculture and Fisheries, Government Buildings, Epsom Road, Guildford, or on request the past statistics from 1953-1966 can be made available for use at the Public Records Office, Chancery Lane, London, W.C.1. Parish statistics have some snags since farm and parish boundaries do not necessarily coincide. This is discussed in "The Cartographic Representation of British Agricultural Statistics", Coppock, J. T., *Geography*, **50** part 2, No. 227, April 1965.

Similar statistics for Scotland are produced by the Department of Agriculture and Fisheries for Scotland, *Agricultural Statistics 1965*, 37½p. Parish statistics for 1965 and earlier are available at the Historical Search Room of the Scottish Record Office, and photostat or microfilm copies of individual sheets, for which a small charge is made, can be provided by arrangement. Enquiries should be addressed to the Curator of Historical Records, H.M. General Register House, Edinburgh 2.

Generalised statistics for the countries of the United Kingdom are given in *Agricultural Statistics*, Ministry of Agriculture, Fisheries and Food, H.M.S.O. These are not so useful as the county figures although they do go back to 1955.

Details of the structure of agriculture classified by Standard Man Hours and types of farming are given in Ministry of Agriculture, Fisheries and Food, *The Structure of Agriculture*, H.M.S.O. 1966 and *Farm Classification 1964-1965*, H.M.S.O. 1967.

More detailed economic statistics giving details of profitability are given in *Farm Management Handbook* published by the Economics Department of Bristol University for the West Midland Region. *The Farm as a Business*, a Handbook of Standards and Statistics, Ministry of Agriculture, H.M.S.O. 1957, gives many examples of costing in farming which will be useful if any cost efficiency studies are undertaken.

Generalised figures of farming, production, yields, and tenure are given in *A Century of Agricultural Statistics 1866-1966*, H.M.S.O. 1968, 87½p.

For world information the following are extremely useful—

F.A.O. *World Crops Statistics 1965*. This gives production of crops by countries.

F.A.O. *The State of Food and Agriculture*—contains statistical review of world agriculture.

F.A.O. *Report on the 1960 Census of Agriculture*—gives very detailed statistics, country by country, including yields, acreages, number of holdings, mechanisation, use of fertilisers, etc.

Transport

Timetables are excellent sources of information for traffic flows and indices of accessibility, see Chapter 7.

BUS. *A.B.C. Coach Bus Guide*, Thomas Skinner, St. Alphage House, Fore Street, London, E.C.2, contains details of all bus companies, maps of all the main coach routes, and maps showing the areas and routes covered by each company. There are numerous timetables of services on the main routes.

Company timetables generally have route maps and maps of the terminals.

ROAD GOODS. *A.B.C. Goods Transport Guide, Motor Transport*. Contains a list of all the regular road services classified in town order, a list of machine carriers by towns, lists of heavy haulage by county, tanker services by towns, and international services by country of destination.

ROADS. Details of road mileages, number of vehicles by counties, types of roads being built, numbers of passengers and amount of freight carried on the roads are given in the Ministry of Transport *Highway Statistics*, published annually.

The movements of goods, their type according to industry, and movement in and out of the standard regions and the type of the commodity carried by all means, and the routes they followed are shown in Ministry of Transport *Statistical Paper No. 6, Survey of Road Goods Transport 1962: Final Results, Geographical Analysis* and *No. 5 Commodity Report*.

Ministry of Transport *Passenger Transport in Great Britain*, H.M.S.O. 1965 gives details of transport movement by air, rail, road, shares of mileages by the different means of transport, the details of passenger transport by rail, public services, road vehicles, and passenger transport by private road vehicle. Details of the number of vehicles licensed are given in the *Annual Abstract of Statistics*. Similar details are given in the *Year Book of the Motor Industry of Great Britain*.

Analyses of the movement of people to and from work and the means of transport used are given in the Workplace and Transport Volume of the 1966 *Sample Population Census*, H.M.S.O.

RAILWAYS. Apart from the timetables produced by each of the regions of British Rail, *i.e.*, Eastern, London Midland, North Eastern, Scottish, Southern, and Western which are rather complicated, the *A.B.C. Rail Guide* and *Hotel Guide*, Skinner, gives details, alphabetically, of every place in Great Britain and its rail connections to London. For places within 70 miles of London complete details are given. Other timetables include Ferry Services in the United Kingdom and to the Continent and timetables of all the narrow gauge railways.

Cooks Continental Timetable, Thomas Cook & Son, Ltd., Berkeley Street, London W1A, 1EB—published monthly, has a map of the railways of each country it deals with and timetable details. In addition there are details of train services. The countries include France, Holland and Belgium, Switzerland, Italy, Spain, Portugal, Scandinavia, Germany, Austria, E. Europe, U.S.S.R., and the Near East.

Full foreign timetables may be seen at a good reference library or perhaps obtained from the London Headquarters of the railways or from foreign embassies. For the purposes of these studies the timetables of the Dutch and Swiss railways are the most suitable because the keys have English translations.

Canadian National Railways, 17 Cockspur Street, London, S.W.1.

Canadian Pacific, 62/65 Trafalgar Square, London, W.C.2.

French Railways, French Railways House, 179 Piccadilly, London, W.1.

German Federal Railway, London House, Finsbury Square, London, E.C.2.

Italian State Railways, 10 Charles II Street, London, S.W.1.

Netherlands Railway, 58 Old Compton Street, London, W.1.

Nigerian Railway Corporation, 9 Northumberland Avenue, London, W.C.2.

South African Railways, South Africa House, Trafalgar Square, London, W.C.2.

Swiss Federal Railways, 1 New Coventry Street, London, W.1.

AIR TIMETABLES. The individual companies have their own timetables which are available from most travel agents. Details of all timetables are given in *A.B.C. World Airways Guide*, published by Thomas Skinner & Co., St. Alphage House, Fore Street, London, E.C.2.

Air cargo details are given in the *A.B.C. Air Cargo Guide and Directory* which includes a list of all the air charter companies, of scheduled services from each town, and the freight charges.

British Airports Authority, *Report and Accounts*, H.M.S.O.

SHIPPING. Shipping timetables cover a much more varied type of vessel and service than those formerly discussed, and formal timetables are not readily available. The shipping companies may provide details of their individual timetables. The most useful is the *A.B.C. Shipping Guide*, publishers Thomas Skinner & Co., which gives a consolidated sailing list, a timetable of the main services and an index to all the world cruises and round voyage operators, gives an index to ports of call and duration of the journeys.

Lloyds List, published weekly, is an alphabetical list of ports of destination, the docks from which they sail, etc. Similar books are *The Handy Shipping Guide*, 12-16 Layshall Street, London, E.C.1., which gives lists of ports and the vessels sailing to them.

The South Wales Shipping List British Transport Docks provides information about the South Wales ports and of the vessels that have arrived at them and sailed from them.

The Port of Manchester Sailing List, Hotspur Publishing Company, provides information for Manchester, and *The Southampton Sailing List*, *British Transport Docks*, provides similar information for Southampton.

RAILWAYS. Ministry of Transport, British Railways, *Board Statistics* gives details of rolling stock, mileages, passengers, etc., but the most important source is the *Beeching Report: Re-Shaping of the British Rail Board, Part 1* Report and *Part 2*, Maps. The maps give details of the freight and passenger traffic at each station in the British Isles.

Janes World Railways 1967-68, Sampson Low, is an account of the world's railways, giving numbers of rolling stock, motive power, and maps.

SHIPPING. Ministry of Transport Docks Board *Annual Report and Account*, H.M.S.O. has details of the trade in and out of the ports.

Digest of Port Statistics, H.M.S.O. gives details of the trade of the ports by types of goods and the port of origin.

British Isles

AIR. Air Ministry *Annual Report*, H.M.S.O., has details of the air traffic in and out of the main airports.

Annual reports of the Civil Airports, Birmingham, Manchester, etc., are usually obtainable from the airport manager. They include details of the inward and outward trade.

Other Transport Sources

U.N.O. *Annual Bulletin of Transport Statistics for Europe 1964* (16th year) contains a very detailed account of transport, railway, passenger transport information by country; passenger transport, vehicle transport, international road traffic; relative importance of the principal modes of inland transport; transport by rail in containers; freight railways, road traffic freight and passenger, inland waterways freight with details of traffic on the Rhine and Danube, international transport by sea, tonnage unloaded at the ports, oil pipeline transport, road, railway, and waterway networks, equipment of roads and railways, consumption of fuel by types of vehicle, statistics of goods carried, types of goods and method of transport. This gives a most detailed picture of the transport systems of Europe.

Ports, Dues, Charges and Accommodation, 1966, George Philip, gives details of the trade of most of the world's ports.

O.E.C.D. Maritime Transport, 1967, has a full account of the main shipping movements, the size and age of world fleets and the details of world carriage of bulk materials, oil, coal, petroleum, etc.

The Suez, Panama, Kiel Canal transport, is enumerated separately. Similar information for the years 1900-1965 is given in *Shipping Statistics*, Institute for Shipping Research, Bremen. Especially important are the details of fishing fleets, trade by goods and areas, world trade by commodity, and details of the vehicular ferries and whaling fleets.

Ports of the World, Benn, contains details of the world ports, including the latest traffic figures.

Population

Yearly figures for local authority areas are available in General Register Office, *Annual Estimate of the Population of England and Wales and of Local Authority Areas*. This gives boundary changes and the estimated mid-year population of England and Wales by local authority areas.

The annual censuses have been published at ten year intervals since 1801. The information contained in the censuses was added to from census to census, *e.g.* the 1881, 1891, and 1901 censuses have full details of the place of origin of the population.

The 1961 Census is published in numerous volumes. *The County Tables* are perhaps the most useful, containing population figures for each Local Authority Area for 1931-1961 including ward populations and areas, the age structure of the population and details of the household arrangements. Migration Tables give the number of immigrants and emigrants by local authority area and by place of origin, and by socio-economic groups. Details of whole industries for the British Isles are given in the Industry Tables. Occupation Tables for each county, give details for each industry and for each administrative area over 50,000. The movement of commuters from their place of residence to their place of work can be worked out from the *Usual Residence Tables*. These give details by the number of people living in one area and working in another. From 1971, details of income are to be included.

The newly introduced five year sample census, 1966 gives similar information based on a 10% sample. The *Work place and Transport Tables*, Vols I and II, give details of transport by train, bus, car, tube, goods vehicles, motorcycles, pedal cycles, and others.

Population figures for European Countries and population structure are given in *Population Structure in European Countries*, U.N.O. International Labour Office.

Yearbook of Labour Statistics, U.N.O. International Labour Office, Geneva, published annually, gives very detailed information of the labour supply, country by country throughout the world.

Industry

Employment figures for industry are given in the County Occupation Tables listed above, and normally the local Employment Exchange will give the figures for the home area.

The Department of Employment and Productivity Gazette, published monthly by the Department of Employment and Productivity, gives much information, including employment figures, wage rates, unemployment figures.

The Regional studies by the Department of Economic Affairs and the Ministry of Housing provides details of employment, changes of employment, employment as compared with the rest of Great Britain, population, transport, housing facilities, etc. They contain excellent information for regional geography. The main studies are:—

Department of Economic Affairs.

West Midland Economic Planning Council, *The West Midlands*, H.M.S.O., 1965.

North West Economic Planning Council, *The North West*, H.M.S.O., 1966.

Northern Economic Planning Council, *The Challenge of the Changing North*, H.M.S.O. *Problems of Merseyside*, H.M.S.O.

South West Economic Planning Council, *Region with a Future*. (In addition to the usual information it contains details of coastal shipping.)

East Midlands Economic Planning Council. *East Midlands Study*, H.M.S.O.

Ministry of Housing and Local Government. *South East Study*, H.M.S.O., 1965.

Yorkshire and Humberside Economic Planning Council. *A Review of Yorkshire and Humberside*, H.M.S.O., 1966.

Yorkshire and Humberside Economic Planning Council. *Halifax and the Calder Valley*, H.M.S.O., 1968.

Figures of industrial production for England and Wales as a whole by industry are given in the Census of Production. The latest one is 1963 and consists of 133 parts, some of which have not yet been published. Volumes 2-129 are the separate industry reports with full details of the industry, labour, wages, etc.

A simplification of these figures for each year is given in the Annual Abstract of Statistics.

Figures of fuel consumption are given in the Ministry of Power, *Statistical Digest*, H.M.S.O., 1966. The British Steel Corporation, *Monthly Digest*, H.M.S.O., £1.05 per year, contains monthly and annual summaries of production by district and also details of raw materials by district. One section deals with production in the other major steel producing countries of the world—Australia, Austria, Belgium, Luxemburg, Canada, France, Germany, Italy, Japan, Netherlands, India, Sweden, U.S.A.

Basic statistics of production, population, trade, etc., are given for the European Common Market Countries in E.E.C. *Basic Statistics of the Community, 1967.* Also useful is *Annual Yearbook* of the E.E.C. Associated Countries.

Commercial Directories published by trade papers or organisations can be used to investigate the British and sometimes foreign patterns in industries. Details of factories, sometimes the numbers of men employed, importers, exporters, suppliers of raw materials, and machinery, are generally given.

Examples are:—

Skinner: *Cotton Trade Directory of the World*—published annually.

                Carpet Trades Annual—published by British-Continental Trade Press Ltd., 220 Strand, London, W.C.1.

                Kompass Publishers Ltd, R.A.C. House, Lansdowne Road, Croydon, Surrey.

See also:—

Oliver, J. L. "Directories and their use in Geographical Inquiry" *Geography*—**49** No. 225, Part 4, November 1964.

Towns

Population and transport information has been detailed above. Information about the commercial structure of the towns, the number of shops of each type, their number of employees, and business, number of hotels, places of entertainment for all places with over 20,000 people in the U.K. are given in the volumes of *Census of Distribution*, Vol. 3-13 and the area tables. The Censuses for 1950 and 1960 are available. The 1950 Census of Distribution is in one volume.

For the correct positioning of shops and industries, the Kelly and similar town directories are available. They may be slightly out of date but are reasonably accurate, and used with a town plan can avoid a lot of time-consuming field work. They give street directories with the names of all the residents and a Commercial Directory, with the addresses of the factories. Kelly's Directories are produced by Kelly's Directories, Eden Street, Kingston-upon-Thames. Town Guides are also useful but not so complete, and obtainable from the Town Hall or Town Council Offices, and sometimes a nominal charge of about 10p is made.

APPENDIX II

USEFUL SYMBOLS AND FORMULAE USED IN THIS BOOK

Useful Symbols

$\sqrt{n}$ is the square root of n.

$(n)^2$ is the square of n.

Σ is the sum of.

$\bar{x}$ is the mean of the x values.

$(n)^{-1}$ is a reciprocal value of n.

$(2)^{-1}$ is equal to $\frac{1}{2}$.

Formulae

1. To determine the standard error in evaluating samples either S.E. $= \sqrt{\dfrac{p \times q}{n}}$, where p is the percentage of land in a given category and q is the percentage not in this category, n being the number of points in the sample. Page 13.

   or S.E. $= \sqrt{\left(\Sigma x^2 - \dfrac{(\Sigma x)^2}{n}\right)\dfrac{1}{n}\cdot\dfrac{1}{n-1}}$

   where n is the number of items and where values of x represent the values of these items. Page 58.

2. To estimate the intensity of farming through the distance index between farms in a study area:

   $$\text{D.I.} = 1.07\sqrt{\dfrac{\text{Total Area Involved}}{\text{Total number of Farms}}}$$

   Page 15.

3. To obtain the location quotient of a square within a study area:

   $$\text{L.Q.} = \dfrac{\text{Number of Employees in Square 1}}{\text{Total Number of Employees in Area}} \times 100$$

   Page 28.

4. To determine the degrees of specialisation within an area:

   Index of Specialisation $= \sqrt{p_1{}^2 + p_2{}^2 \ldots p_n{}^2}$

   where p is the percentage of people employed in industry 1. Page 29.

5. To determine the activity rate:

   $$\text{Activity Rate} = \dfrac{\text{Number employed}}{\begin{array}{c}\text{Total Population}\\\text{of working Age}\end{array}} \times 100$$

   Page 30.

6. To determine the density of points in a study area:

   $$\text{Density} = \dfrac{\text{Number of Points}}{\text{Area}}$$

   Page 37.

7. To calculate the expected mean in a random distribution:

   $$\text{Expected Mean} = \dfrac{1}{2\sqrt{\text{Density}}}$$

   Page 37.

8. To determine the degree of randomness of a distribution:

   $$\begin{array}{c}\text{Degree of Randomness}\\(RN)\end{array} = \dfrac{\begin{array}{c}\text{Observed or Measured}\\\text{Mean}\end{array}}{\begin{array}{c}\text{Expected Mean in a Ran-}\\\text{dom Distribution}\end{array}}$$

   Page 37.

9. To determine the rank size rule relationship of town n to the primate city: $P_n = P_1 (n)^{-1}$ where P_n is the population of town n, P_1 is the population of the primate city, and n is the rank size of town n. Page 41.

10. To determine the breaking point for retail trade between towns located in a predominantly rural area (Reilly's Law of Retail Gravitation)

    $$\begin{array}{c}\text{Distance of Breaking}\\\text{Point from smaller}\\\text{Town } B\end{array} = \dfrac{\text{Distance in miles } A\text{-}B}{1 + \sqrt{\dfrac{\text{Population } A}{\text{Population } B}}}$$

    Page 45.

11. To determine the relative attraction of retail trade by towns in a more urbanised area (Urban Case of Reilly):

    $$\dfrac{\text{Volume of } A\text{'s Retail Trade to } B}{\text{Volume of } A\text{'s Retail Trade to } C}$$

    $$= \dfrac{\text{Population } B}{\text{Population } C} \times \left(\dfrac{\text{Distance } A\text{-}C}{\text{Distance } A\text{-}B}\right)^2$$

    Page 47.

12. To estimate the probability of shoppers living in Centre 1 using Centre 1 as opposed to other centres within the study area by applying Huff's Probability Model:

$$\text{Probability of C 1} = \frac{\dfrac{\text{Number of Shops in Centre 1}}{\text{Time taken or Distance travelled to reach them}}}{\dfrac{\text{Total number of shops in the Study Area}}{\text{Total time taken or Distance travelled to reach them.}}}$$

Page 47.

13. Formula for the Spearman Rank Correlation Coefficient:

$$r = 1 - \frac{6\,\Sigma d^2}{(n^3 - n)}$$

where r is the coefficient of correlation, d is the difference in ranking, and n is the number of items ranked.   Page 54.

14. Formula for the Pearson Product Moment Correlation Coefficient:

$$r = \frac{\Sigma\,xy}{\sqrt{\Sigma x^2\,\Sigma y^2}}$$

where r is the coefficient of correlation and x and y represent values of the two variables being correlated.   Page 55.

15. To determine the shape index of an area:

$$\text{Shape Index} = \frac{\text{Length of the Longest Axis}}{\text{Length of the perpendicular to the boundaries of the area midway along the longest axis}}$$

Page 61.

16. To determine the integration of a network (the Beta Index):

$$B = \frac{\text{Number of Edges}}{\text{Number of Vertices}}$$

Page 63.

17. To estimate accessibility within an area by determining an index of directness:

$$\text{Index of Directness} = \frac{\text{Road Distance}}{\text{Direct Distance}} \times 100$$

Page 65.

18. To estimate the volume of movement between towns by using a simple gravity model:

$$\text{Movement } A\text{-}B = \frac{\text{Population } A \times \text{Population } B}{(\text{Distance } A\text{-}B)^2}$$

Page 69.

Guidance in the Use of Random Numbers:

1. Both the horizontal and vertical grouping of the numbers may be ignored. This printing arrangement is merely to facilitate use.

2. Numbers may be used in any combination: either singly, or in twos or in threes. Examples:
   i. To establish a six figure grid reference use threes, e.g. 201742.
   ii. To choose a random sample from numbered items not exceeding 100 use two figures, e.g. 20. Note in this case that 00 would represent the hundredth item.

3. Numbers may be used in sequence either vertically or horizontally provided use is consistent. For example, in establishing the grid reference one may choose either 201742 or 201744.

4. Once the direction of movement has been determined, i.e. either vertical or horizontal, this must not be varied.

5. The initial choice of numbers may take place at any point in the table, e.g. row 20 and column 9 would be 4. The above rules about choice of combination and sequence of movement thereafter must be observed.

TABLE OF RANDOM SAMPLING NUMBERS

20 17	42 28	23 17	59 66	38 61	02 10	86 10	51 55	92 52	44 25
74 49	04 49	03 04	10 33	53 70	11 54	48 63	94 60	94 49	57 38
94 70	49 31	38 67	23 42	29 65	40 88	78 71	37 18	48 64	06 57
22 15	78 15	69 84	32 52	32 54	15 12	54 02	01 37	38 37	12 93
93 29	12 18	27 30	30 55	91 87	50 57	58 51	49 36	12 53	96 40
45 04	77 97	36 14	99 45	52 95	69 85	03 83	51 87	85 56	22 37
44 91	99 49	89 39	94 60	48 49	06 77	64 72	59 26	08 51	25 57
16 23	91 02	19 96	47 59	89 65	27 84	30 92	63 37	26 24	23 66
04 50	65 04	65 65	82 42	70 51	55 04	61 47	88 83	99 34	82 37
32 70	17 72	03 61	66 26	24 71	22 77	88 33	17 78	08 92	73 49
03 64	59 07	42 95	81 39	06 41	20 81	92 34	51 90	39 08	21 42
62 49	00 90	67 86	93 48	31 83	19 07	67 68	49 03	27 47	52 03
61 00	95 86	98 36	14 03	48 88	51 07	33 40	06 86	33 76	68 57
89 03	90 49	28 74	21 04	09 96	60 45	22 03	52 80	01 79	33 81
01 72	33 85	52 40	60 07	06 71	89 27	14 29	55 24	85 79	31 96
27 56	49 79	34 34	32 22	60 53	91 17	33 26	44 70	93 14	99 70
49 05	74 48	10 55	35 25	24 28	20 22	35 66	66 34	26 35	91 23
49 74	37 25	97 26	33 94	42 23	01 28	59 58	92 69	03 66	73 82
20 26	22 43	88 08	19 85	08 12	47 65	65 63	56 07	97 85	56 79
48 87	77 96	43 39	76 93	08 79	22 18	54 55	93 75	97 26	90 77
08 72	87 46	75 73	00 11	27 07	05 20	30 85	22 21	04 67	19 13
95 97	98 62	17 27	31 42	64 71	46 22	32 75	19 32	20 99	94 85
37 99	57 31	70 40	46 55	46 12	24 32	36 74	69 20	72 10	95 93
05 79	58 37	85 33	75 18	88 71	23 44	54 28	00 48	96 23	66 45
55 85	63 42	00 79	91 22	29 01	41 39	51 40	36 65	26 11	78 32
67 28	96 25	68 36	24 72	03 85	49 24	05 69	64 86	08 19	91 21
85 86	94 78	32 59	51 82	86 43	73 84	45 60	89 57	06 87	08 15
40 10	60 09	05 88	78 44	63 13	58 25	37 11	18 47	75 62	52 21
94 55	89 48	90 80	77 80	26 89	87 44	23 74	66 20	20 19	26 52
11 63	77 77	23 20	33 62	62 19	29 03	94 15	56 37	14 09	47 16
64 00	26 04	54 55	38 57	94 62	68 40	26 04	24 25	03 61	01 20
50 94	13 23	78 41	60 58	10 60	88 46	30 21	45 98	70 96	36 89
66 98	37 96	44 13	45 05	34 59	75 85	48 97	27 19	17 85	48 51
66 91	42 83	60 77	90 91	60 90	79 62	57 66	72 28	08 70	96 03
33 58	12 18	02 07	19 40	21 29	39 45	90 42	58 84	85 43	95 67
52 49	40 16	72 40	73 05	50 90	02 04	98 24	05 30	27 25	20 88
74 98	93 99	78 30	79 47	96 92	45 58	40 37	89 76	84 41	74 68
50 26	54 30	01 88	69 57	54 45	69 88	23 21	05 69	93 44	05 32
49 46	61 89	33 79	96 84	28 34	19 35	28 73	39 59	56 34	97 07
19 65	13 44	78 39	73 88	62 03	36 00	25 96	86 76	67 90	21 68
64 17	47 67	87 59	81 40	72 61	14 00	28 28	55 86	23 38	16 15
18 43	97 37	68 97	56 56	57 95	01 88	11 89	48 07	42 60	11 92
65 58	60 87	51 09	96 61	15 53	66 81	66 88	44 75	37 01	28 88
79 90	31 00	91 14	85 65	31 75	43 15	45 93	64 78	34 53	88 02
07 23	00 15	59 05	16 09	94 42	20 40	63 76	65 67	34 11	94 10
90 08	14 24	01 51	95 46	30 32	33 19	00 14	19 28	40 51	92 69
53 82	62 02	21 82	34 13	41 03	12 85	65 30	00 97	56 30	15 48
98 17	26 15	04 50	76 25	20 33	54 84	39 31	23 33	59 64	96 27
08 91	12 44	82 40	30 62	45 50	64 54	65 17	89 25	59 44	99 95
37 21	46 77	84 87	67 39	85 54	97 37	33 41	11 74	90 50	29 62

Each digit is an independent sample from a population in which the digits 0 to 9 are equally likely, that is each has a probability of $\frac{1}{10}$. (Reproduced from *Tracts for Computers*, *No.* 24. Department of Statistics, University College, London.)

SUBJECT INDEX

AUTHOR INDEX

PRINTED IN GREAT BRITAIN BY UNIVERSITY TUTORIAL PRESS LTD, FOXTON, NEAR CAMBRIDGE

ARABLE LAND

- Cereals
- Ley legumes
- Roots
- Green fodder
- Industrial crops
- Fallow

MARKET GARDENING

- Field vegetables
- Mixed market gardening
- Nurseries
- Allotment gardens
- Flowers
- Soft fruit
- Hops

ORCHARDS

- With grass
- With arable land
- With market gardening

GRASSLAND

WOODLAND

- Deciduous
- Coniferous
- Mixed
- Coppice
- Coppice with standards
- Woodland scrub

WATER & MARSH

- Water
- Freshwater marsh
- Saltwater marsh

HEATH, MOORLAND, ROUGH LAND

UNVEGETATED

SETTLEMENT

- Commercial & Residential
- Caravan sites

OPEN SPACE

- Tended but unproductive land

INDUSTRY

- Manufacturing
- Extractive
- Tips
- Public utilities

TRANSPORT

- Port areas, airfields, etc.
- Major roads
- Other metalled roads

DERELICT LAND

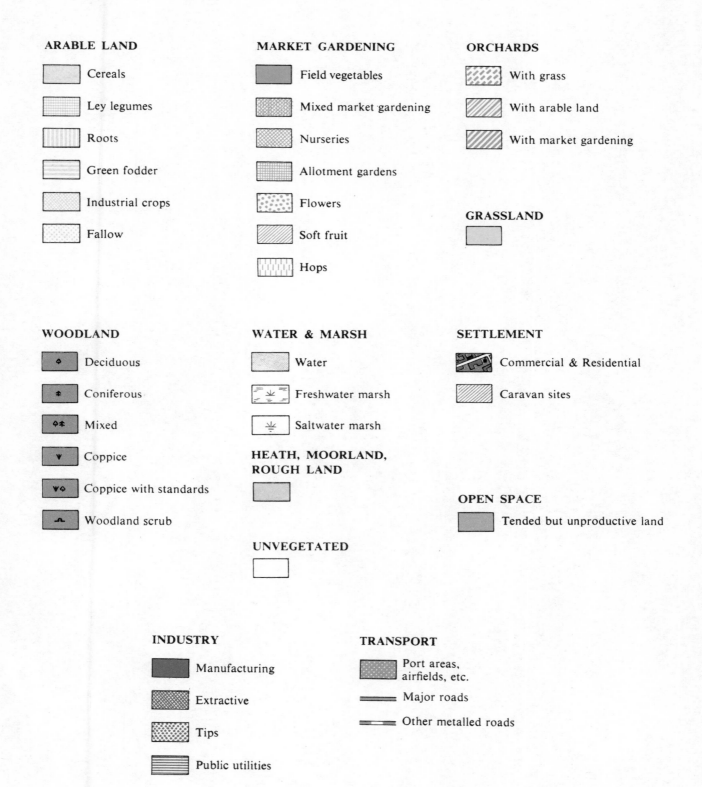